The
EVERYTHING®
Kama Sutra Book

Dear Reader:

It has been fascinating writing this book. I thought I knew quite a lot about the Kama Sutra but I found myself enthralled with what I *didn't* know. I have always loved trying new positions and I have had a willing partner to help along the way. The Kama Sutra is so much more than positions, though.

The depth with which the culture that produced the Kama Sutra looked at all aspects of life and integrated them is impressive. It created a philosophical ideology that included the study of sexuality as a science, which was openly debated between scholars, sages, religious persons, and society alike. Taught by those who knew it best, sexuality was honored.

I have studied Tantric philosophy and neo-Tantric techniques for many years. I have been a part of spiritual circles, run businesses, raised three daughters, held my father in my arms while he died, traveled all over the world, written books and articles, and produced films, yet something about this particular journey has been different. I have finally created the solid realization that there are ways to live in the world that bring spirit, harmony, and right-livelihood together. *The Everything® Kama Sutra Book* literally flowed out of me, inspired by the ancient texts that are included in it. It has been an exquisite experience for me, on multiple levels.

In love and gratitude,

Suzie Heumann

The EVERYTHING® Series

Editorial

Publishing Director	Gary M. Krebs
Managing Editor	Kate McBride
Copy Chief	Laura MacLaughlin
Acquisitions Editor	Eric M. Hall
Development Editor	Patrycja Pasek-Gradziuk
Production Editor	Jamie Wielgus

Production

Production Director	Susan Beale
Production Manager	Michelle Roy Kelly
Series Designers	Daria Perreault
	Colleen Cunningham
Cover Design	Paul Beatrice
	Frank Rivera
Layout and Graphics	Colleen Cunningham
	Rachael Eiben
	Michelle Roy Kelly
	John Paulhus
	Daria Perreault
	Erin Ring
Cover Artist and Interior Illustrator	Susan Kaye

THE
EVERYTHING
KAMA SUTRA
BOOK

Unlock the ancient
secrets of erotic expression—rediscover
passion and enhance intimacy

Suzie Heumann

Adams Media
Avon, Massachusetts

To my partner, lover, and fellow adventurer, Michael.

An Everything® Series Book.
Everything® and everything.com® are registered trademarks of F+W Publications, Inc.

Published by Adams Media, an F+W Publications Company
57 Littlefield Street, Avon, MA 02322 U.S.A.
www.adamsmedia.com

ISBN: 1-59337-039-3

Printed in the United States of America.

J I H G F E D C B

Library of Congress Cataloging-in-Publication Data
Heumann, Suzie.
The everything Kama sutra book / Suzie Heumann.
p.   cm.
(An everything series book.)
ISBN 1-59337-039-3
1. Sex. 2. Love. 3. Sexual intercourse. 4. Vatsyayana. Kamasutra.
I. Title. II. Everything series.

HQ31.H47483 2004
613.9'6–dc22

2003023146

Illustrations courtesy of Susan Kaye.

This book is available at quantity discounts for bulk purchases.
For information, call 1-800-872-5627.

Contents

Acknowledgments

A profound thank-you to the ancient adventurers who explored, advanced, and transformed lovemaking to a high art form. Seeing the act of making love as a spiritual journey and an intimate bonding experience was a groundbreaking cultural step. Its reverberations are being felt today, more than ever.

Top Ten Ways the Kama Sutra
Can Spice Up Your Love Life

1. Introduce variety into your love life through new exotic positions.

2. Integrate deep intimacy techniques to enhance all of your relationships in life.

3. Become a master at maximizing your orgasmic pleasure.

4. Learn to enhance and amplify your seductive qualities.

5. Discover the soul and spiritual aspects of great sex.

6. Bring out the essence of the god/goddess in your lover.

7. Expand your erotic potential by exploring the erogenous zones of your bodies.

8. Learn the science of kissing and foreplay.

9. Create love ceremonies to transform your lovemaking experience.

10. Discover the G-spot and ejaculation mastery for men.

Introduction

▶ THE NAME "KAMA SUTRA" conjures the image of exotic passion and erotic skills from the past. The old illustrations and fine art paintings depict couples in ecstatic positions with their bodies naturally aligned. We believe that they had something that we don't have today. This is true; they had a love manual to top all love manuals. Created by many scholars, in the oral tradition, over thousands of years, the Kama Sutra has come to us today by sheer grace. It could have been lost forever except for an ingenious Englishman in the 1860s, who translated it and brought it to the West.

The ancient written version of the Kama Sutra is attributed to a man named Vatsyayana, who said it best when he wrote: "Texts on the science of Kama (pleasure) are of help only until passion is excited; but once the wheel of passion begins to roll, there is no sutra and no order." The society that studied, taught, and created the Kama Sutra texts knew that every young couple would need help if they were ever to get to a place where sexuality became a high art form for them. It was a culture that honored the sciences, religious duty, and family. It also honored the science of sex, which was seen as a high art form. It was considered necessary for a good citizen to be knowledgeable in sexual techniques, caring, compassion, and relationship skills.

The text excerpts from the original Kama Sutra are interesting in and of themselves. The original is written in "sutra" form: short verses, or aphorisms. This allows the space for a teacher to help interpret for new students. It is also perfect for a modern book on the subject because the original texts support the idea of a teacher adding an infusion of examples, details, and new applications.

The Everything® Kama Sutra Book is filled with exercises, activities, knowledge, and fun possibilities. It covers a wide variety of positions, expanding orgasmic pleasure, and the art of seduction. It details the many arts that a citizen in the times of the Kama Sutra was expected to study, and draws important comparisons to today's citizen.

The Everything® Kama Sutra Book also explains the different types of bodies we have and how best to make them fit together. Kissing and erotic touching techniques are explored, as well as enhancement techniques that will take the practitioner to an even higher state of ecstasy. Relationships, aphrodisiacs, and lovers' emotions are also covered here. You can even learn how to dance an exotic dance for your lover, if you so desire.

The whole text of the original Kama Sutra has not been covered here because some of it does not apply in today's world. For example, harems aren't common, though some men may like to fantasize about them, and other detailed entries held no pertinent information for this particular book. Regardless, the book is overflowing with playful, vulnerable, and insightful ideas to bring more joy into your relationship and your lovemaking.

Each one of us is responsible for his or her own sexual happiness. It isn't our lover's responsibility, though it is wonderful if we feel partnered with someone who wants to have sexual happiness, too. *The Everything® Kama Sutra Book* is designed to give you and your partner a lifetime of knowledge and creative ideas to help you have the most fulfilling sexual experiences life can bring. Ⓔ

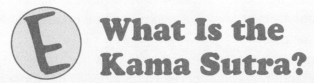

Chapter 1

What Is the Kama Sutra?

The classic Eastern love manual, the Kama Sutra, is perhaps the most sought-after reference to sexuality of all times. Translated and brought to the West in the 1800s, it supplied a set of guidelines that helped everyone in ancient India come to a similar understanding of their erotic nature. In modern times, the Kama Sutra began its most popular era in the 1960s, during the so-called sexual revolution. Today, it remains more popular than ever.

The Parts of the Kama Sutra

The Kama Sutra is a manual on conducting relationships between lovers. Best known by Westerners for its variety of exotic sexual positions, the Kama Sutra has as much to offer modern couples as it did their counterparts in ancient India. Though some of its parts aren't pertinent to contemporary lovers, here is an overview of how the original sutras were written and divided. A majority of these sutras will be covered in detail in the body of this book.

- **General Remarks:** The beginning (Part 1) addresses the three aims in life: the obtainment of wealth (Artha), the rules and morals of behavior (Dharma), and the erotic practices to assure pleasure and the existence of life itself (Kama). It also addresses the learning and the acquisition of knowledge, conduct, and intermediaries for the lover.
- **Amorous Advances:** This section (Part 2) is the one that most of us know as the sexually detailed area. It describes positions, embraces, biting, oral sex, caressing, scratching, stimulation, desire, the behavior of women, and conducting a lovemaking session.
- **Courtship and Marriage:** This part (Part 3) details courting rituals and includes topics such as relaxing the woman, ways of convincing the woman to agree to courtship, and the forms of marriage.
- **Duties and Privileges of the Wife:** This area (Part 4) addresses both the situation of only one wife in the household and many wives within the residence. It details how the wives should conduct their lives, and offers psychological suggestions for the harem's peace and happiness.
- **Other Men's Wives:** This part (Part 5) examines the conduct for having an affair with another man's wife. The use of an intermediary is discussed, along with how to set up an encounter.
- **About Courtesans:** This is an extensive section (Part 6) dedicated to the courtesans. The section outlines ways in which they should conduct their lives and business affairs. It details whom they should take as a customer, what they should do in the acts of love, and how to manage long-term lovers.

- **Occult Practices:** Aphrodisiacs, spells, and potions are covered here (Part 7), as well as remedies for impotency and low libido. Plants, herbs, spices, and other products of the time are also mentioned.

A Universe of Eroticism

Due to a renaissance of interest in sexuality, personal growth, and spiritual seeking, the Kama Sutra is gaining new acceptance as it grows older. Western cultures don't have anything to rival the Kama Sutra. The erotically positive cultures of the past understood that sexuality was part of a healthy lifestyle. Pleasure, sensuality, and sexuality add happiness, fulfillment, and even more years to our lives.

The Kama Sutra supplied a set of guidelines that helped everyone in ancient India come to a similar understanding of their erotic nature. The need for this deeper understanding in the West fuels our attraction to this great treatise on the nature of human intimacy.

FACT

"Kama" means pleasure or sensual desire. It is the name of the Indian God that represents the sexual nature in man. "Sutra" means short books or aphorisms.

The Kama Sutra is much more than a manual of positions, though this is a very important component of it. The detail that is brought forth in the world's greatest love manual is done so with the attention of the scientist. The observations on men's and women's erotic and emotional nature are forthright and deep.

The overall variety and depth of information in the Kama Sutra ranges from detailed kissing techniques to seduction and courting suggestions. It explores the idea of biting your lover to leave your mark on him or her. The instructions on scratching techniques are for the same purpose and to heighten the sensual feel of the skin during lovemaking. Thrusting techniques are mentioned. Some of the positions are named after animals, for this was one of the ways to study man's relationship with the natural world.

◀ A stone sculpture from ancient India

The Kama Sutra also describes many different techniques to stimulate the senses, including the ten types of "blows" and the sighs that accompany them. It details the way in which a man might grasp his lingam (penis) and churn it from side to side in the yoni (vagina) of his lover. It outlines the areas in the yoni to stimulate and has special names for the sides, top, deep areas, and the entrance. You'll get the sense that the Kama Sutra was indeed considered a science.

Eros, the ancient Greek God of Love, is equivalent to Kama, the Hindu God of Love. Psyche, Greek for soul, is the Greek counterpart to Shakti, the supreme Hindu Goddess.

The Culture of Ancient India

Understanding the culture of India in the time of the original Kama Sutra will help you with some of the more biased portions of the texts. They may be considered biased because at the time the Kama Sutra was written down some men had multiple wives and some of the "erotic" practices might border on abuse in today's culture. Though we won't delve deeply into the parts of the texts that don't fit our modern society, it is instructive to know a little bit about the society from which these ideas came. Even today, many aspects of the Indian culture have seen little change.

India was divided into feudal-like states and provinces in the fourth century A.D. when the Kama Sutra was condensed and written down. Kings controlled the states. Ministers and officials helped conduct the business of the province. Merchants and traders were educated and traveled widely.

The Caste System

The caste system was fully represented in the India of Vatsyayana. One did not associate with members of another caste, let alone marry someone who was either below you or above you in life's station. Generally, it was the upper, or Brahman, caste that studied the sutras and lived according to them. All the castes except the "untouchables" were encouraged to study the sutras and lead good, moral lives.

QUESTION?

Who are the "untouchables"?
The "untouchables," or pariahs, are individuals who are at the bottom of or outside the Hindu caste system. The Indian political and religious leader Mahatma Gandhi gave the untouchables the name *Harijans*.

Upper-class citizens appear to have known good hygiene and had a detailed knowledge of medical remedies and health care. Women knew how to concoct hair color treatments, makeup, and potions for many uses. Astronomy, Ayurvedic medicine, yoga, meditation, and the sciences were all well-established disciplines.

Spiritual and Cultural Scriptures

Spiritual and cultural scriptures came in the form of sutras or, in earlier days, "shastras." These included the Artha Shastra, the Dharma Shastra, and the Kama Shastra, among others. These documents contained the information that society held sacred. A well-bred, conscientious man or woman was expected to lead their life according to these scriptures. It is believed that the Kama Sutra was condensed from the original Kama Shastra, which contained 1,000 chapters! Vatsyayana distilled the information to its current size and left couples and teachers to "read between the lines" for interpretations.

FACT

The Chinese invented paper around the time of Christ, but it wasn't introduced to India until the fifteenth century A.D. The sutras and scriptures were written on palm leaves before that, and even today, many ancient texts must be rewritten to preserve them from deteriorating.

The Four Aims of Life

The Kama Sutra is part of an overall, complete picture of life that the ancient Hindus understood. Extensive writings, in the form of other sutras, were available on many subjects and were part of the well-bred citizen's life. Included in this were good health practices, the attainment of knowledge, an understanding of the universe and its workings, and the ritual honoring of the gods and goddesses.

On the acquisition of obtaining Dharma, Artha, and Kama:

"Man, the period of whose life is one hundred years, should practice Dharma, Artha and Kama at different times and in such a manner that they may harmonize together and not clash in any way. He should acquire learning in his childhood, in his youth and middle age he should attend to Artha and Kama, and in his old age he should perform Dharma, and thus seek to gain Moksha, i.e. release from further transmigration. Or, on account of the uncertainty of life, he may practice them at times when they are appropriate to be practiced. But one thing is to be noted, he should lead the life of a religious student until he finishes his education." — Part 1, Chapter 2, the Kama Sutra

The citizen held most important the first three of four aims in life; Artha—the accumulation of wealth; Kama—the knowledge and advancement of pleasure; and Dharma—the practice of worship and of having high moral standards. The fourth—Moksha—was the attainment of enlightenment and liberation from the cycle of death and rebirth. Being excellent at the first three assured the fourth.

Artha

The attainment of Artha meant that it was a citizen's moral duty to be comfortable in life and be able to support a family. The acquisition of material goods and the pursuit of economic interests was one of the main objects of life and included arts, land, gold, cattle, wealth, equipment, and friends. This was particularly true for the merchant classes and the traders. It was believed that you couldn't pursue the other two well if you were worrying about being able to feed your family or offer money contributions to the local temples.

ALERT!

Artha, the accumulation of wealth, should be learned from the king's officers, and from merchants who may be versed in the ways of commerce. So says the scriptures of the times.

Kama

To attain Kama one had to pursue the desire for erotic pleasure. Kama is the enjoyment of appropriate objects by the five senses of hearing, feeling, seeing, tasting, and smelling, assisted by the mind together with the soul. The sutras held the belief that sexual pleasure was one of the most enjoyable things man could do. It is the foundation from which we all came and was to be revered and sought after. Being sexually knowledgeable was a high duty not only for procreation, but for bliss and pleasure.

It was not to be indulged in to the point of ignoring the other aims in life, though. Many scholars believed that without Kama a person would not have the drive to pursue Artha or Dharma. This can certainly be seen when a married couple is about to have a child. The nesting instinct to provide for the family and child takes over and that drive is what causes the pursuit of the other aims in life.

Dharma

Dharma means "right conduct" and includes virtue, righteousness, and truth. It is thought to be the most important of the three aims of life that lead to the fourth, Moksha. If there is ever a conflict of the three aims in life, then Dharma is said to be the one to follow. Cosmic and natural laws were seen as the highest paths of knowledge. Faith, devotion, and kind deeds were the actions to support the Dharma path.

Moksha

A basic tenet of Hinduism is the cycle of birth, death, and rebirth according to Karmic actions during a lifetime. Moksha is the liberation from this perpetual wheel, sooner rather than later. During a lifetime, if the person lives up to the three aims of life and sets a very fine example for themselves, they will shorten the cycle of Karmic action and move faster to the place of final resting—Nirvana.

Can you evaluate yourself according to the demands of a citizen of ancient India? What score would you give yourself in the areas of Artha, Dharma, and Kama? Think about this and be honest and objective. Are there areas that you would like to improve in your life?

Ancient Sages and Modern Scholars

The written form of the Kama Sutra came from a long history of rich oral tradition. Writing had disappeared in India about 3,500 years ago with the advent of the Aryan invasions. Around 600 to 700 B.C. the ancient manuscripts were again written down in the Sanskrit language. Though the original "rules of love" were attributed to Nandi, the god

Shiva's companion, it was a man named Babhravya who compiled the vast manuscripts of earlier days into a more manageable work some time between the seventh and eighth centuries B.C. There were 1,000 chapters in the original work by Babhravya, called the Kama Shastra.

Vatsyayana

A scholar named Vatsyayana is attributed with the Sanskrit version that we know today. He wrote this condensed version from the original Kama Shastra around the fourth century A.D. The Kama Sutra was meant as a guide to be memorized and to have the more subtle points shown through interpretation of a lover or guide.

Therefore, its structure appears as poetry and verse. The descriptions of the positions, morals, and guidelines are short and to the point. It's almost as if they were meant as reminders to the couple, rather than as detailed instruction. In that way they can be remembered, until they become habit, during the early years of sexual relations.

Sir Richard Burton

The Kama Sutra is perhaps the best known of all the love manuals. It came to modern society when an Englishman named Sir Richard Burton translated it from Sanskrit in the middle 1800s. Burton was an intrepid adventurer and is credited with helping to discover Lake Victoria and the head of the Nile River, among other accomplishments. It is also believed he spoke forty languages fluently.

The sexual mores in Victorian England during his life were very restrictive. Because Sir Burton traveled extensively, he may have experienced some of what is contained in the Kama Sutra firsthand. Other scholars of the subject understand that he was generous with his interpretations rather than staying within a strict translation.

FACT

The Kama Sutra shocked Victorian England, and after Sir Richard's death, his wife burned many of the other books he had translated. Most of them have not been retranslated and indeed many may be lost forever.

Contemporary Scholars

In the last century there have been several important people in Western society who have helped reintroduce the erotic arts of the East into mainstream Western cultures. Alain Danielou, Nik Douglas, and Penny Slinger, among others, have been instrumental in translating for us the intricacies and subtleties of the ancient practices. They have molded the teachings, in the tradition of true teachers, to modern tastes.

Alain Danielou, renowned musician, racecar driver, singer, sportsman, traveler, and scholar, was born in Paris in 1907. He lived in India for many years. He studied the vina, a classical Indian string instrument, and became adept at Sanskrit and the Hindu culture.

◀ A stone sculpture from the erotic temples of India

In 1963, Alain Danielou returned to Europe with the intent of bringing Indian and Asian culture to the West. Since that time, he has written more than twenty books on Indian culture. Two of his more recent books deal with the profound effect westernization has had on the rich Indian culture. He sees the loss of the divine and the connection with nature that the Hindu culture has suffered at the hands of becoming "modern."

Nik Douglas and Penny Slinger created the book *Sexual Secrets* in the early 1970s. It is still the contemporary "bible" to the Kama Sutra and Tantra, a mystical path that employs sexuality as a vehicle to enlightenment. Through Nik Douglas's scholarly words and Penny Slinger's incredible artwork, the Western world began to grasp the concepts put forth in the Kama Sutra. Their active participation and deep understanding has opened up these insights for modern men and women.

The Other Kama Sutras of the World

After A.D. 400, a series of "books" or aphorisms appeared in several predominant Eastern cultures. These books were manuals on lovemaking. They included guides for couples on kissing, touching, positions in lovemaking, attitudes, moral obligations, and much more.

The *Perfumed Garden*

The *Perfumed Garden* was written in Arabia in the sixteenth century. It has a treatise on the many different sizes and shapes of penises and vaginas (*lingam* and *yoni* in Sanskrit). Accordingly, it details thirty-five types of lingams and thirty-eight types of yonis. Written primarily for men, it counsels them to ask the woman for instruction on giving her pleasure. It also contains teaching stories of various sorts and many intercourse positions.

The Ananga Ranga

The Ananga Ranga was written in the sixteenth century in India. It details morals, seduction techniques, sexual positions, hygiene, rituals and sexual spells, aphrodisiacs, and other erotic concepts. It pays particular attention to the woman learning to control her pelvic floor muscles to heighten the experience between her lover and herself.

The *Secrets of the Jade Bed Chamber*

This treatise on sexuality and sensuality includes recipes for potency remedies, exotic positions, and counseling on the ways of love. As with many societies that included eroticism in their cultural heritage, there is symbolism in the words selected for use in the books and by lovers.

A Jade Stalk meant a man's lingam, whereas a Jade Garden refers to the woman's yoni.

Metaphors about the ways of love are used extensively in Eastern cultures; some are amusing while others are erotic and secretive.

The *Ishimpo*

The *Ishimpo* was a manual that originated in Japan as the erotic teaching manual for that culture. Similar to its counterparts in India and other parts of Asia, it depicted the sex act between man and woman as the essential force that controlled the universe. It expressed the importance of making love as the force in nature that keeps the earth circling the heavens.

Pillow Books

China, Japan, and most Eastern cultures had what are termed "pillow books" in addition to the teaching manuals mentioned here. These books were used by couples as erotic stimulants and as reminders of a human's vast sexual potential. They could be used when a couple got into a rut in their sexual and sensual relating. Pillow books were adorned with beautiful erotic pictures, poetry, writings, and suggestions that couples could consider together to stir their passions.

The Role of the Teacher

The sutras—whether the Artha, Dharma, or Kama Sutras—were written as aphorisms or short sayings so that they could be both memorized and taught and interpreted by a qualified teacher. The author's interpretation, or alternatively one by a scholarly associate, always accompanies contemporary versions of the translations. The language that the sutras are written in is often difficult for the layperson to understand, and the added help of additional teachings and commentary further the meaning of the information contained therein.

While the young lovers and students of the past enjoyed the opportunity to have a teacher to work with on the finer points of the Kama Sutra, people today may not always have that chance. As you read this book, help your lover and have him or her help you understand the subtler points. Act as each other's teacher so that you may both enjoy the delicious fruits of the love chamber. Guide and gently hold your lover in the arms of the gods and goddesses, and the centuries of lovers before you who have traveled the path of Kama, the God of Love.

Chapter 2

The Kama Sutra for Modern Lovers

Without a manual of our own, we have turned to the East to educate us on the ways of love. We're interested in the exotic, erotic maneuvers that the Kama Sutra brings us. Western societies have never developed a science around sensuality and sexuality, but it's recognized that there is a need for it. What better place to look than the beautiful, erotic pages of the Kama Sutra.

Why Are We Interested?

Our sexual nature is an important part of life, yet it has often been relegated to behind-the-door furtive acts that leave us frustrated, unfulfilled, and wanting more. As a society, we fantasize about cultures of the past and romanticize their relationship to love and the erotic arts. But we lack support in learning the arts of making love, and need a culture that encourages the sexual acts as a form of art. New generations see the Kama Sutra as the literary work that holds this promise.

Western Curiosity of World Cultures

The world is getting smaller and smaller through better communication and efficient methods of transportation. The influences of many cultures are beginning to blend borders between countries, and our knowledge is increasing about things that weren't available to us before.

Sex sells things in Western cultures, but the fact that we actually *have* sex has been kept underground until very recently in our history. We're only just now coming out of our Victorian-like mindset about our sensual natures and our innate sexuality. We need a manual that provides us with the basic lessons by which to guide our explorations into the pleasure and bliss of sexual intimacy.

ALERT!

The Kama Sutra was never meant to encourage promiscuity or sexual indulgence. Just as a little liquor adds a pleasant euphoria but too much leads to intoxication, knowledge of the sexual acts and arts enhances the act but doesn't give license to debauchery.

The 1960s Opened Doors

In the middle to late 1960s, the so-called "sexual revolution" opened the doors for many people to explore their sexual nature more fully. Indian culture was beginning to come to the West in the form of yoga, Ravi Shankar's music, madras shirts, incense, and Indian-imported clothing. The Beatles were meeting with gurus in India, and the Kama

Sutra was being put into modern book form for the first time. The ways of the East showed a new path to an area of life that the West had pushed under the covers, literally.

New Sources and Interpretations

The Kama Sutra was designed in short aphorisms so that couples could remember them and teachers could assist students in learning their finer points. The same is true today. Every book, instructional film, or love manual on the Kama Sutra places the author in the role of the teacher.

The Kama Sutras are a rich combination of the original words, and the knowledge that we have today of the body, the workings of the mind, and the understanding of psychology. Included in that body of knowledge is the relatively newfound freedom that Western women, as well as men, have gained in recent years.

India Then and Today

Today's modern India is a product of Western thought and institutionalism, and is very similar to the United States and most of Europe. Though India primarily follows the Hindu faith, and not Christianity, it aspires to being—and is rapidly becoming—very westernized. It prides itself on this fact and continues to move farther away from its heritage of a sublime mix of science, spirit, and sexual freedom.

Women in India's History

India was, for most of its history, very progressive toward women, sexuality, the arts, and culture. Women had a lot of power and responsibility in the time of the Kama Sutra, as men relied on them for their opinions and thoughts on a variety of both everyday problems and worldly affairs. Most wives were, however, confined to the home compound, and women could not appear in public places unless an older woman or a male relative accompanied them. Whereas most courtesans could study the arts of love, as well as the many arts that were listed in the *Sixty-Four Arts*, including the sciences, commerce, languages, and music, married women had to seek permission from their husbands before engaging in worldly affairs.

FACT

The Sanskrit word *Madana* means "love" or "sexual love."
The word *Madanalaya* means "the female sexual organ."

Modern India

Today's India has a large middle-class population that aspires to Western-style living conditions. Women work outside the home in all professions and manage to raise the children too, as in the past. The computer sciences have taken India by storm and have produced numerous companies and brilliant individuals who have played a great role in the rapid advancement of technology in both the East and the West. The travel industry is booming in India, as well. Tourists from all over the world are drawn to this country by its interesting history, culture, and Eastern teachers and gurus. India has much to teach the West, yet the Kama Sutra and sexuality are what bring many to its doors.

Times Have Changed

As revered as the Kama Sutra is today, many of its parts just don't fit modern society. Most civilizations around the world—both Western and Eastern—don't consider it appropriate to have more than one wife, but that was not true in the days of the Kama Sutra. In fact, much of the work includes details on how to handle multiple wives, and even lovers and courtesans.

Outdated Concepts

There are many things in the Kama Sutra that no longer fit both our modern sensibilities and our cultural beliefs. Though women did have a strong presence in some aspects of their lives in India, the equality of the sexes was nothing like we know today. And even though sexism still exists today, the line dividing equal opportunity between the sexes is thinning. From jobs to orgasms, women are claiming their territory with passion.

Portions of the Kama Sutra put the man's needs first and tend to have a male "voice." This makes sense since a man wrote it. Some of the sections, like the one on scratching, seem to imply that rather severe scratching and biting serve to "mark" the woman. The idea that she is "taken" by a very passionate man comes to mind.

The Issue of Polygamy

Kings often had many wives but wealthy civil servants, traders, and merchants might also take more than one wife if they could afford it. The Kama Sutra describes, in detail, both the responsibilities of the wives and the man of the household. In another part, it even goes as far as to say that a wife neglected or beaten by her husband has every right to find another lover—and is actually encouraged to do so. Here are some interesting passages from the part of the Kama Sutra that describes such issues:

- "At festivals, singing parties, and exhibitions all the wives of the king should be treated with respect and served with drinks" (Part 4, Chapter 2, Sutra 82).
- "The women of the harem should not be allowed to go out alone, nor should any women outside the harem be allowed to enter except those whose character is well known. And, the work of the king's wives should not be too fatiguing" (Part 4, Chapter 2, Sutra 83).
- "A man marrying many wives should act fairly toward them all. He should neither disregard nor pass over their faults, and should not reveal to one wife the love, passion, bodily blemishes, and confidential reproaches of the other. No opportunity should be given to any one of them of speaking to him about their rivals, and if one

of them should begin to speak ill of another, he should chide her and tell her that she has exactly the same blemishes in her character" (Part 4, Chapter 2, Sutras 85–87).

- "He should learn to please all of his wives in different ways. One of them he should please by secret confidence, another by secret respect, and another by secret flattery, and he should please them all by going to gardens, by amusements, by presents, by honoring their relations, by telling them secrets, and lastly by loving unions" (Part 4, Chapter 2, Sutras 88–89).
- "A young wife who is of a good temper and who conducts herself according to the Dharma Shastras wins her husband's attachment, and obtains superiority over her rivals" (Part 4, Chapter 2, Sutra 90).

Multiple Partners

It appears as though men with many wives sometimes made love to several of them at once. This would take a lot of stamina to satisfy all of them. There are recipes in Chapter 18 that recommend potions to be taken by men who must perform this daunting task. Courtesans were also employed for this unusual pleasure activity.

ALERT!

Many people, especially men, interpret the Kama Sutra as being a guide and open license for orgies. This is not true. It was designed for couples as a spiritual guide to accomplish the third aim in life—that of Kama.

Some of the beautiful eleventh-century sculptures on the temples in the village of Khajuraho, India, depict several combinations of multiple partners during lovemaking. It is believed that some show multiple women because of two different scenarios. The first is the situation of many wives or courtesans being involved in an erotic adventure. The second is that often the handmaidens of a royal woman might be involved in helping the couple shape themselves into difficult amorous positions. They might help support the woman's legs or be available to bring the couple food and drinks, or to play music for their enjoyment.

▲ A harem scene

The Presence of Courtesans

Courtesans were revered and an honored part of society in ancient India, indeed in many cultures around the world, both Western and Eastern. Their company was sought out, and they were the only women who could actually be seen in public at gatherings and community events. They were highly educated in current events, languages, the arts and sciences, and especially in the art of love.

The Fine Details of Being a Courtesan

The Kama Sutra contains exhaustive details for courtesans. It describes the methods by which courtesans should make money, what lovers they should take, and even how to get themselves out of debt and problems. "According to Vatsyayana, the principle reasons for becoming a courtesan are: Material gain, escape from physical or financial dangers, and the love for a particular person" (Part 6, Chapter 1, Sutra 18).

FACT

In Sanskrit, *Garika* means "a courtesan who is pious, liberal, and devoted." A *Kumbhadasi*, on the other hand, means "a courtesan whose aim is the acquisition of wealth, physical comfort, and an easy life."

The Kama Sutra also describes who should become a courtesan, how she should go about doing it, and what qualities she should possess. In addition, the Kama Sutra recommends that the wives should—with permission from their husbands—learn the arts of love (and as many of the other arts as possible) in the event that their husband dies and they then must support themselves. Here's a list of qualities a courtesan was expected to have:

"The qualities desirable in a courtesan herself are: Beauty, youth, marks on her body proving her good fortune, sweet speech, appreciation of virtues and accomplishments of the young man, not undue fondness of material gain, desire for love and physical union, consistency of mind, honesty and frankness in her dealings, ambition for acquiring extraordinary accomplishments, generosity, and appreciation of the Arts and of social gatherings. But the most common qualities which courtesans actually possess are: Intelligence, character, good behavior, honesty, gratitude, foresightedness, absence of inconsistencies, awareness of the properties of time and place, refined way of life, and expert knowledge of the science of love and its ancillary arts. They possess the absence of begging, loud laughter, speaking ill of others, citing faults of others, anger, covetousness, disrespect of the things that are to be respected, fickle mindedness, and interrupting other's speech." —Part 6, Chapter 1, Sutras 13–14

A Courtesan's Value

Courtesans imparted a feeling of confidence in the men who courted them. They seemed to have an honored place in the best of society. They employed the help of friends and even their mothers to find good clients and trustworthy confidants. Very often one courtesan would have only a few lovers in her lifetime and be very close to them. But, the sages said, that if she wanted to be wealthy, she had to have many lovers of the highest quality. "The following list shows the value of payment in order of preference: Gold, silver, copper, bronze, iron, bedstead, blankets, silk cloth, perfume or sandalwood, chilies, furniture, ghee, oil, corn, and cattle" (Part 6, Chapter 5, Sutra 7).

◀ A courtesan playing and dancing

Spiritualism

The spiritual aspects of the Kama Sutra are threaded throughout the text and refer to the many aspects of love and the regenerative powers of sex. The Kama Sutra is born from the trinity of the three aims in life: wealth, pleasure, and good karma. As mentioned in Chapter 1, these lead to an afterlife that shortens the cycles of death and rebirth, and allows the citizen to reach heaven in a more direct path.

The Hindu Creation Myth and Kama

According to the Hindu mythological creation story, nymphs called *apsarases* served Kama, the God of Love. They carried his emblems, or symbols, which were the fish, the conch shell, and the lotus flower—all elements that come from an association with water.

Water is considered life giving, and it is a symbol of creativity and our sexual nature. These are all aspects of the second chakra—the sexual chakra. The lotus is also a deep symbol associated with the yoni, or the vagina. It is a regenerative symbol of life.

An ancient and most famous Tantric mantra goes thus: "The Jewel is indeed within the Lotus." The inference is that the Jewel is the seed, or semen, and that the Lotus is the yoni. According to the mythological creation story, the world and all of the gods were created and born from the Lotus, the womb of the mother.

◀ Symbolic lingam in the yoni—ritual object

Universal Symbols of Fertility

Shells have been associated with marriage and fertility from early times. The Greek goddess Venus came from a shell and rose out of the ocean foam. Spring is the season of Kama. The fertility and fecundity of this time of year cannot be denied. Many pagan religions had ceremonies that were centered on fertility rites during spring. It is also said that it is in the springtime of your life that you are most interested in Kama.

Our Sensual Senses

Our lives rely on our senses, and the arts that we study in life rely on them as well. The Kama Sutra teaches that it is the senses that should be followed in order to instruct us in reaching life's fullness. They are not to overrun our sensibilities, but are to be followed and recognized as guides on the path to our sexual nature.

The Kama Sutra teaches about using the senses to get more out of life. The Indian culture, for example, has a highly developed culinary sense. It loves and promotes the arts, including music, dance, and painting. The landscape of India is even visually stunning. The music is very advanced and the ceremonies surrounding religious duties are highly artistic and refined. The senses are alive and well in India, even today. The Kama Sutra played artfully on this essence of life.

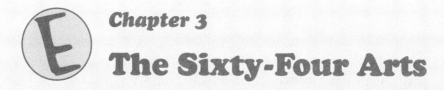

Chapter 3

The Sixty-Four Arts

The Sixty-Four Arts are an integral part of the Kama Sutra, and there are two sets of them: the arts that augment education and life, and those that pertain to lovemaking. The Kama Sutra focuses on the lovemaking set, but mentions the other because they were a means to make one's self more attractive.

The Inner Beauty

The author of Kama Sutra, Vatsyayana, reveals that the cultivation of inner beauty was just as important as nurturing outer beauty. Attractiveness comes from a refined and imaginative mind as much as it does from darkened eyes, ruby lips, and a fine figure. Therefore, cultivating as many of the arts other than the art of lovemaking was of great importance to society.

Most of us do indeed follow life pursuits or interests that are as varied as the number of people in the world. You may play an instrument, write poetry, paint, sing, or participate in any number of personal interests that fuel your creative side. It is those pursuits that the ancient sutras believed made us all more attractive individuals.

Men, but especially women, were encouraged to learn as many arts as possible. Refinement and accomplishment were important and many of the arts were not gender specific. These arts included music, singing, sciences, lovemaking, homemaking, poetry, dance, shooting of the bow and arrow, conversation, sewing, art, games, magic, chemistry, perfumery, and rituals.

Who Studied the Arts and Sciences?

Gender differences during the time the Kama Sutra was written, and even in some societies today, dictated that the sexes learn some of the same things. Obviously, they also had a gender-specific education. Can you imagine a merchant of the times learning the art of bed making? Not likely, so learning high arts of the home and family was actually a woman's responsibility. Conversely, few women enjoyed the freedoms of being businessowners.

"Man should study the Kama Sutra and the arts and sciences subordinate thereto, in addition to the study of the arts and sciences contained in Dharma and Artha. Even young maids should study this Kama Sutra along with its arts and sciences before marriage, and after it

they should continue to do so with the consent of their husbands"
(Part 1, Chapter 3).

FACT

The exception to this rule was the courtesan. She was considered a businesswoman; she was expected to know the wiles of a woman, the arts of love, and to have a top-notch business savvy too.

Teachers of the Kama Sutra

For various reasons, including the chastity of the young woman student, it was thought that only select persons should teach the finer points of the Kama Sutra. In the case of a woman, that person would need to have the confidence of the girl and her family, and have her best interests at heart. It is especially true because often this teacher might also act as the go-between in a love match for the young student.

Male Versus Female Guide

The Kama Sutra addresses the case of the young woman more so than of the young man. As seems true today, young men have permission to be their own go-between for arranging instruction and practice in the arts of lovemaking. Men were more worldly at the time and could arrange for schooling in the sciences, business, and politics. Comparably, a young woman led a much more secluded and sheltered life.

ESSENTIAL

The Kama Sutra suggests that a girl should study with a confidential friend who can be trusted. Her teacher could be any one of the following persons: the daughter of a nurse who was brought up with her who is already married; her aunt on her mother's side; a female friend who can be trusted; an older female servant; or her own sister.

Art Categories

The Sixty-Four Arts listed here have been put into a rough order that classifies them according to categories. They aren't necessarily in their original order, but you will understand them better and see the relationships they have with each other more effectively this way. It may be instructive, if you are so inclined, to take an active role in learning something from each of the categories.

Musical Arts

The musical arts were very important to the times in ancient India and elsewhere in the world. Clearly, there were no televisions, radios, car stereos, or MP3 players. Musical arts were highly regarded and very entertaining. They included:

- Singing
- Playing of musical instruments
- Dancing
- Blending dancing, singing, and playing of musical instruments
- Playing on musical glasses filled with water
- Theater and stage setups

You have probably experienced the essence of an erotic song or dance in your lifetime. Can you remember being swept away by the rhythm, the beat, and the words? You can feel in your body when something is erotic. There will be "movement" of a sort that is hard to describe but is definitely there. Paintings from the Kama Sutra era often depicted dancers and musicians; frequently, the woman was the musician and she may even have been playing the lute while she was making love. Talk about music!

While a person today might still be accomplished in many of these things, some other unique items could be added to this list. How about karaoke, singing in a choir, playing an electric piano that mimics 200 instruments or a whole band, or computerized sounds created without a human voice. Playing music and singing songs are grand forms of communication that have changed little in thousands of years.

◀ The art of making music

Social Arts

The social arts were important in a world that was fairly conservative and not nearly as cosmopolitan. The arts of conversation and storytelling created a pleasant passage of time for most people. Cultures with oral histories told tales or used ballads that could be simple entertainment, or relayed parables that had underlying messages for the good of society. They could be teaching stories, erotic tales, tales of desire, and tales of love lost.

FACT

The great goddess Sarasvati from the Hindu pantheon is the goddess of music, dance, singing, the arts, and learning. Great temples have been built to honor her and she is always represented as a beautiful woman with grace and character. Her statues are often seen in modern households.

The famous story of Shaherazad, who told 1,001 stories in as many nights, is an example of powerful storytelling. The king who held her ransom was so taken by her exotic stories of heroes and heroines that he kept her alive, night after night, to entertain him with yet another tale. Though she was from Arabia, her life was similar to that of her contemporaries in ancient India.

Here are the social arts that the Kama Sutra lists as subjects to be studied:

- Writing (both poetry and prose)
- Conversation
- Cordial relations with relatives
- Storytelling
- Playing of games
- Hunting and the shooting of the bow and arrow

You'll notice that hunting and shooting are on this list. At the time of the Kama Sutra's writing, hunting was deemed necessary because wild tigers and lions were frequent cohabitants with the human population. To hunt with a bow and arrow was a great social skill and showed prowess. Ancient paintings depict hunting even while making love.

◀ Combining the arts was a special practice.

Practice Storytelling

The art of storytelling has practically disappeared today. Just think about how thrilled you are with the rare fiction writer who can take your breath away. There is a small but growing segment of contemporary erotic writers, who are capturing our imagination with their writing. Check online or at your favorite bookseller for erotic stories to read with your lover. Trust and develop your own skills as a storyteller. A good story or joke teller these days makes a party a whole lot more fun. Practice the art of telling stories to your partner and see where it gets you.

ALERT!

Modern Westerners are not as gifted in these social arts as the people in the time of the Kama Sutra. Games today tend to be played alone, on the computer screen, rather than on the veranda with friends. Playing erotic games with your lover is a good way to get creative again with game playing.

Worship Arts

Participating in the rituals and ceremonies of the Hindu culture created a fine sense of the artistic qualities of worship, both in men and women. In modern-day India, people can be seen cleaning, adorning, and anointing the statues of the gods and goddesses numerous times a day. The practice of honoring their religious idols creates a whole set of wonderful arts that move the spirit and add joy and connectedness to life. Some of these are:

- Adorning a statue of a god or goddess with rice cakes and flowers
- Arranging flowers upon the ground for a procession or holy day
- Stringing flowers for garlands and wreaths
- Conducting rituals
- Understanding the sutras, and other holy books and manuscripts

Many modern Western religions have some ritual aspects to them. We celebrate birthdays and a few holidays, but by and large, we are not a culture that creates ceremonies for everyday living. Understanding and participating in some kind of spiritual art form might add tremendous value to peoples' lives today. Simply saying a statement of gratitude when you put the flowers your lover brought you in a vase is a wonderful way to start.

In Bali, Indonesia, rituals are apparent in every walk of life. During any day of the week you'll see a young man's very clean motorcycle strewn with handplated wreaths and flower decorations. He might tell you that he appreciates his transportation and is honoring it.

Celebrating Life with Rituals

You might want to think about ways to bring more meaning and small rituals into your life. Setting up an altar with a flower and some incense or a candle can be a wonderful reminder to say a prayer of gratitude every morning. This might also be a place where you can meditate a few minutes each morning. Starting your day this way adds grace and beauty to the rest of the day and brings serenity to your life.

Though most of us would not make rice cake offerings to our religious icons, we might study the art of Ikebana (flower arrangement) or bonsai (bonsai tree planting). You may offer your home to your family at holidays and decorate it to show the festivity of the season. You may even honor the solstices and equinoxes by offering seed for the wild birds or by bringing flowers to friends. These are all rituals that fill our lives with meaning and fill the hearts of those we love.

Researchers report that many modern women are very interested in bringing more ceremony into their lives. Creating blessing ways (a Native American tradition) for life passages, such as birth, marriage, and death, can help families and friends stay connected.

How about creating a love ritual every year at Beltane, which is the spring pagan time of fertility? You and your lover could go away together for a romantic holiday or stay at home and create a long, luxurious ritual that is all yours. Don't be intimidated or shy about this. You only have a playful and creative time to gain from it, let alone some erotic fun.

Personal Arts

High on the list of the personal arts is the art of lovemaking. The pursuit of Kama, or pleasure, was considered a religious duty for the procreation of children and the fulfillment of sexual pleasures. This ensured a happy, healthy lifestyle so that the citizen would then attend to the duties of the other aims in life, those of accumulating wealth and living a moral life.

Besides the art of lovemaking, personal arts included drawing and painting, tattooing and applying henna, stringing beads for necklaces, spreading and arranging beds or couches of flowers, making ear ornaments, creating and preparing perfumes, sewing adornments in dressing, and binding men's turbans and chaplets.

◀ The art of lovemaking

In ancient India, both men and women explored the arts of drawing and painting, but most of the old Kama Sutra paintings come from male artists. The erotic nature of the arts is represented on the temples at Konarak, Khajuraho, and Varanasi, in the form of beautiful rock carvings of couples. The application of henna to the hands and feet of women was a high art that is still seen today. Many people in the West have also adopted the wearing of henna on arms and ankles.

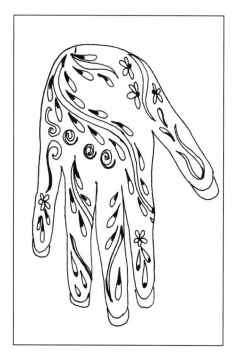

◀ The art of body adornment with henna

Homemaking Arts

The homemaking arts were and are today some of the most important things an individual can learn. You may not have to manage water resources in your home, but creating comfortable, inviting areas where your family can entertain friends, cultivating a garden, or pursuing the culinary arts may excite you. Consider picking something from this list and learning how to do it. You may also wish to create your own list of homemaking arts that interest you.

- The art of making beds
- Picture making, trimming, and decorating
- Quickness and manual dexterity
- Culinary arts including preserving and cooking
- Storing and managing water resources
- Making lemonades, drinks, and spirituous extracts
- Herbology and plant uses
- Gardening and growing food and flowers

You probably buy most of your life necessities and accessories from a store. Many people work outside their homes and don't have time to experiment with creating their own concoctions, like perfumes or lotions. Yet, some individuals attend classes and go to workshops to learn just these things.

Herbal classes are offered in many large and small towns where a man or a woman can learn to make his or her own creams, lotions, perfumes, body and massage oils, and even herbal medicines. A great variety of books are available with excellent resources—from ingredients to recipes. These activities can be a source of relaxation and pride for individuals who want to renew their roots to a more traditional creative spirit. These are practical and worthwhile additions to any person's life.

Science Arts

In ancient India, many of these arts appealed to men more than to women. For example, language arts came in handy for a merchant or trader. Knowledge of the stars and astrology was needed for finding auspicious dates for conducting business deals or for sailing merchant ships. Knowledge of medicines and healing techniques was also popular among the men, as was education about other cultures. Despite being considered "man's domain," the science arts, however, did not exclude courtesans, who were often as highly educated as men in the ways of the world. They were sought after for their knowledge and womanly wisdom in such matters.

Ayurvedic medicine and healthful living was a high art form in India, which had some of the most advanced remedies and techniques known at that time. It was a whole-body system that included yoga, meditation, and cleanliness. Knowledge of chemistry was necessary and a little sorcery was helpful, too!

Current Trends in the Arts

Many of the sciences on the list of the Sixty-Four Arts are antiquated and inappropriate for individuals today. Though there are obvious parallels, it's easy to come up with new items that are of interest to the modern man and woman. What do you enrich your life with? Here are some additions for the modern citizen's list:

- Coaching teams for children's leagues or adult sports.
- Body sculpting or exercising at the gym.
- Going on family vacations with activities like fishing, hiking, and boating.
- Participating in extreme sports.
- Taking part in educational and recreational travel to distant parts of the world.
- Collecting and preserving antiques.
- Doing carpentry and home repair.

The Arts in Your Life

Cultivating and developing yourself, in many different ways, adds to your quality of life and will enhance your sense of self. Artistry is in everyone. Improving your dexterity and your sense of sight, sound, taste, and touch, while in the creative mode, helps improve neural function and cognitive abilities.

If you are inclined to learn a new art, don't censor your first tries. Be open to taking the time to create and develop in your new art form. The point is to have fun, even in the lovemaking arts, and not to do it perfectly.

You may want to try a new type of artistic endeavor with your partner. Consider starting a garden together or landscaping a section of your outdoor living space as a joint project. Design and implement a new tiled entranceway to your front door or run a race for charity together. Create something and see how you do with it. Find ways to be partners rather than a leader and a follower. Create Kama, pleasure, and enjoyment in the activity.

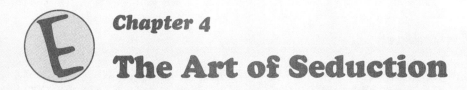

Chapter 4

The Art of Seduction

Seduction is truly an art form. Some people do it well, while others need a little help. Confidence is the underlying factor of seduction, and you'll need to practice to get your confidence up. Seduction can include how you dress, your behavior, flirting techniques, truth telling, exotic dancing, communication techniques, and more.

Seduction

Seduction can involve the use of all the senses in life and the art of love. You don't need to be turned off to it because you think it is coercive or manipulative. Telling the truth can be very seductive, if you do it right. You can develop your own unique brand of seduction, and if you think you already have it, you can refine it to work for you and your lover even better.

Kindness

Showing kindness, compassion, and interest in what your lover is involved with in life is seductive. Everyone loves true attention. There is great seduction in sharing drink, food, words, music, and the things that romance is built around. The Kama Sutra notes that young people are, by nature, generous with themselves and their worldly goods. These qualities attract us to each other.

Flirting Techniques

The Kama Sutra is full of subtle techniques to woo a potential lover. Coyness, sitting by oneself, and glancing furtively at the object of desire are all natural techniques employed by heartfelt lovers to entice a potential mate. Lovers have used actions, such as accidental/on-purpose brushing up against an arm, a breast, or a foot under a table since the beginning of time.

Wittiness is very seductive, and it is a great way to flirt. Knowledge is an excellent way to break the ice when approaching a new person. But being smart shouldn't equate to being snobby. If you are prone to being "a know-it-all," then try to preface your comments so that they become more like a genuine offering rather than a way to make you look good.

ALERT!

Be genuinely interested in what the other person has to say. Listen attentively, especially if that person is a woman. Make eye contact a lot and for extended periods of time. Practice it and add a smile. It doesn't hurt and will actually make you feel better inside even if the person doesn't respond much.

In the days of the Kama Sutra, people used go-betweens to arrange meetings (dates). In a way, that happens today, only on a less formal basis. Being bubbly and vivacious often draws people's attention to you. This has to happen in a natural setting though, because it is easy to spot a person who is forcing a bubbly personality.

Using Sexy Words

For both men and women, words can be powerful erotic stimulators. In general, men will prefer lusty teasing, and more explicitly sexual language. Women tend to respond to more indirect language—hints, words of love and desire, compliments. Regardless of what you like, the idea is to start the erotic play before you get to the bedroom. The longer we can be juiced up, the stronger our reactions will be when we get there.

Don't hesitate to use words liberally when making love. And make sounds to let your partner know how you are feeling. Here are some activities to try, with several different versions. You may want to create new, additional variations that are appropriate for times other than when you are making love. Sit facing each other when you do these. Take turns.

- Give each other the gift of one minute of compliments. Just say as many loving, complimentary words and phrases as come to your mind. Don't think too much—just let them flow out. Switch.
- Take one minute to say as many erotic, hot, sexy words as you can come up with. Don't censor your words—just let them out.
- In one minute, say as many words of compassion, care, and sympathy as come to your mind. Use this one when one or both of you are experiencing hurt or vulnerability.
- Use words of gratitude and thanks for one minute each. This practice helps us remember to speak about how precious our lives are. Use this one generously!
- Make up your own version with themes that fit your life.

Erotic Presence

Erotic presence, the way you radiate your erotic nature, is a key component that is missing for some people. This is not to say that you must become alluring, coy, and seductive, but rather that you become aware of your capacity for natural eroticism. Grace, energy, and confidence allude to an erotic nature. Take the opportunity to notice what your style is and how you might develop it.

Dancing

If you go dancing, try upping the ante a little. Don't worry about technique; consciously throw yourself more fully into the steps and the swing. Be the dance. Let the energy flow through you. If you feel self-conscious about erotic presence, try dancing at home just for yourself. Choose a time and place where you have privacy. For both men and women, you might want to dress in a sarong or something a bit sexy. Find a scarf, a hat, or a feathery boa you can wave around. Put on music with a good rhythm and start to move. Men will usually want something with a good, strong beat. You can dance in front of a mirror if you'd like.

◀ Practice dancing for releasing the spirit.

Let Yourself Go

Don't censor your movement—just let yourself go. Try a new move. Wave your arms around. No one can see you. It will all be good for a little inside joke later, anyway. Keep it light. Loosen your pelvis up with some body waves. To do these, stand with your feet a little apart and bend your knees. Relax. As you begin the movement, stick your bottom out and then gently swing your hips forward. When you feel comfortable with this, begin to let your upper body move to the wave. Your spine will become looser and the wave will move up to your neck and head. Do this slowly and as you repeat it, begin to smooth out the movements. Let your head go and include the natural action of your arms. Go with the flow.

FACT

Doing a body wave is an excellent way to warm up for love-making. You may even get to the place of being able to dance for your lover. Imagine yourself as a temple dancer. What better erotic foreplay could you imagine?

With a little practice, it will become easier for you to let yourself go. You'll begin to notice other areas in your life where you can apply this same idea. The big shift will be apparent in your lovemaking, but beyond that, a sense of erotic presence will energize your whole life. Find opportunities to be graceful and confident. Notice how you might add a bit of spice to that moment—especially if your partner is around to reap the benefits.

Setting the Stage for Love

Take as many of your senses into consideration when setting the stage for love. "Kama is the enjoyment of objects with the help of the five senses—of hearing, of speech, of sight, of taste, and of smell. Kama is that special pleasure experienced when the sense of touch operates, and when it is in contact with the object that generates the pleasure" (Part 1, Chapter 2, Sutras 11–12).

Before making love, also consider the following: "The bed should have a canopy above it, with garlands and bunches of flowers all around. There should be pillows, some at the top of the bed and some at the end. There should also be a separate couch, as well as perfume, musical instruments, fruits, drinks, and games to play" (Part 1, Chapter 2, Sutras 6–12).

The Sense of Smell

Smell is a very erotic motivator. Using aromatherapy and incense are wonderful ways to enhance a room toward the exotic—so are fragrant flowers like gardenias, roses, lavender, carnations, and lilies. Citrus-scented candles are also a delight and they are relatively mild.

Using small amounts of pure essential oils on a light bulb or in an aromatherapy dish, with heat added, is a delicate way to expand the scent in a room. Linen sprays and essential oil mists work well, too. Make sure to use only a small amount—a little goes a long way.

Cleanliness is very important, especially when you are near another person. Avoid the use of heavy, personal perfumes. They can cover up the wonderful natural smells of the body. These subtle smells are natural attractants.

The Sense of Taste

Include things to sip, luscious fruits, chocolates, desserts, and other things when setting up the love room—especially on occasions when you know that you will be spending time at the game of love. You can even incorporate some of the treats into your sexual activities. When together, drink and eat slowly and sensually. Offer each other tidbits, feed each other, and lick each other's fingers.

The Sense of Sound

Most cultured citizens played at least one instrument in the days of the Kama Sutra. They sang, told tales, played music solo and with others, and danced. Music played a major role in the lives of almost everyone.

Listen to more music and find evocative sounds that turn you on. Create a date, with your love, to go listen to and buy some new music together. Pick things that sway your hips, and cause you to undulate and swoon. Drums and deep base sounds along with sitars and other Middle Eastern instruments make excellent music for lovemaking. Belly dance music is erotic and sensual, but try selections from many different genres as well.

Beauty Aids

In the days of the Kama Sutra, people paid great attention to the manner of dress, makeup, cleanliness, and jewelry. The culture prescribed certain requirements for what constituted beauty in those days, much as we do today. The sciences of the time included ways of making makeup, dying hair, and creating exquisite perfumes, among other items.

FACT

Henna tattooing is as popular today as it was then. Brides have elaborate henna designs drawn on their hands and feet. You can see the soles of the feet that are painted red in some of the ancient erotic paintings of the times.

Dressing, Tattooing, and Jewelry

Elaborate forms of dress haven't changed much in thousands of years in India. Although modern women and men do wear Western clothing quite extensively, the sari is still the most common form of attire. The sari is a very long length of beautiful cloth that is wrapped around the torso and the last bit is then thrown over the shoulder. A slip is worn underneath, along with a short-sleeved top that comes to the midriff. Usually a little bit of waistline shows. Many consider this form of dress provocative, but very fitting for a culture that brought us the Kama Sutra.

During the times of the Kama Sutra, jewelry was also considered an important beauty aid. Women put on jewelry in the morning when they got dressed, and there were everyday pieces and more formal and elaborate pieces. Depending on the party, event, wedding, religious festival, or daytime activity, jewelry always had its place and often represented the wealth and status of the individual.

Kama Sutra Beauty Formulas

The last part of the Kama Sutra contains descriptions of things that make one attractive to others. The list of the Sixty-Four Arts contains many items that had to do with beauty, which women were expected to blend and create for their households. They used various blends to color the eyelids, eyelashes, eyebrows, and lips: "Collyrium, in a finely prepared paste with other ingredients, and mixed with the oil of Aksha, is then smeared on a cotton wick and heated over a lamp. When applied to the eye-lashes, adds to the appearance" (Part 7, Chapter 1, Sutra 5).

This part also includes information on hair dyes, breath fresheners, perfumes, and even body pastes used for tightening and lightening the skin. There is a mention of aphrodisiacs, which were also created for the use of the citizen. "Pieces of Vacha smeared with mango juice and preserved for six months in the crevices of a Sinshapa tree-trunk, exude a divine fragrance and may be used as scent in winning over women" (Part 7, Chapter 1, Sutra 31).

◀ A woman with jars of beauty potions

Pillow Books, Erotic Writing, and Games

There are all kinds of ways to interact with your lover instead of, say, going to the movies or watching television. Lovers of the past developed skills at games, theater, acting, joke telling, and conversation because this was the way people passed the time with others. Simple mind games, joke telling, and suggestive writing can be a powerful seducer that doesn't just have to happen behind closed doors.

Reading Erotica

Reading erotic materials to your partner can be exquisitely sensuous. As you read, you can place your own intention and inflection on the sentences you want to emphasize. You can even act out some of the parts and talk about or fantasize about what you are reading together.

Pillow books are books that have pictures, writing, and sometimes instructions—like position books. They provide a great resource for erotic adventure. There were many erotic books, other than the Kama Sutra, that not only brought pleasure but also helped educate whole generations. These books are available today in modern forms and are quite informative as well as evocative and titillating.

In an online survey at ✑ *www.tantra.com*, 26 percent of responders said they never fantasize during lovemaking, 65 percent said they sometimes do, and 9 percent always fantasize. When asked if they involve their partner in the fantasy, 35 percent said they never do, 35 percent said they talk about it, 23 percent have played it out a few times, and 7 percent play it out on a regular basis.

The Art of Writing to Seduce

Writing erotica or words of seduction doesn't have to be difficult. You might say that you can't, but it isn't true. All you need to do is write down what you are feeling at any given moment. Your writing needn't be slick; in fact, it shouldn't be.

There is a great, simple method taught by writing teachers in which you just pick up your pen and write for ten minutes. You don't censor and you don't think. You write anything that comes to mind. If you just sit and feel what it is that is moving you, then the words will flow.

Your lover doesn't care if you're not the best writer. Don't let the fear stop you. Practice a little a few times a week. Throw it away at first if you want to, but keep writing. Then, in the future, when the feeling comes over you, jot a note to your lover.

Here is an example:

My Love,

I am missing you.

I notice my yoni ever so slightly tightening as I think of you and a flood of warmth invades and sweeps over my body. I tighten and relax consciously, all the while thinking of you, inside of me—three shallow, one deep, three shallow, one deep. You gaze into my eyes—you gauge yourself and study me—we are instruments of pleasure—you for me, me for you—us together, dissolved into bliss.

Yearning to hold you,

Suzie

Writing Poetry

Writing poetry has long been a symbol of both romantic and erotic love. Even writers of little skill can successfully write poetry to their lover and have it be received as though it came from a master. The gift of writing from a lover is a gift of time, care, and love. Try writing one poem together, and see what you come up with.

If you are inclined to write a love letter but feel intimidated by it, ask for help at the bookstore. Purchase a book of poetry and sprinkle generously some of the author's words in your letter. It'll turn your partner on in more than one way!

If poetry isn't something that turns you on, consider stretching yourself a little if it is something you think your lover would love. In addition, create love notes during the day and week that point to the anticipation of a particular erotic event that might be planned. Leading up to a date with notes and love letters is an outrageous way to create titillating tension. By the time you get together, you'll be all over each other!

Love Games

Erotic couples played all sorts of games, both of love and sport, in the time of the Kama Sutra. It was a high art to be able to play games successfully, with wit and intelligence. Erotic games were part of the art of seduction.

FACT

You can purchase board games or card games for lovers. Give it as a gift to your partner for the beginning of an erotic evening. Get one that looks good to you and is not too silly. There are some very high-quality games available. Try "Erostrix" from the tantra.com catalog.

Games can be fun, and they can be challenging. Some people will take to them a little easier than others. Simple games can have a unique place in intimate relationships if they are healthy, conscious, and fun. They can teach you new things about your partner. They can gently push boundaries and open new realms. And they can open a Pandora's box full of dark secrets, perceived danger, and adventure.

Know your partner and, if you are going to introduce the idea of games into your love-play, pick ones that will be fun for her and not too confrontational. It's important to remember to respect your partner at all times. If something isn't working for one of you, then stop or change. Create codes like red for "Stop," yellow for "Slow down," and green for "This is great."

Mostly, though, games are fun and a good cause for humor and lightheartedness. They introduce a new approach to sexuality that we don't often come up with ourselves, and they can be cause for opening up the imagination to create your own fun.

The Blindfold Game

Sight is a powerful sense—perhaps the strongest of all our senses. It is the first sense we draw on in everyday life. It is a powerful driver of experience. When we take it away, we give much more control over to our other senses.

This is a blindfold game. It will help you heighten your senses and increase your awareness of touch and sensation. It is designed to be an evening of exploratory fun that will also train the two of you to pay more attention to your other senses.

Find a rose; a piece of very soft fur; a new, small art-style paintbrush; a feather; or anything that will produce a very sensual feel. Have a soft scent in a misting bottle and a gentle bell or chime handy. Gather at least four items but have them reflect as many different senses as you can.

Set the scene by lighting candles, putting on soft erotic music, and having something to smell, and later nibble, close at hand. Strawberries, chocolate, mango pieces, kiwi slices, peach slices, and several selections to drink are a good start. Blindfold your lover.

Now, using your imagination, use each of the items on your partner but ask him or her to identify what it is that you are using. Let him or her smell the food by waving it in front of the nose slowly. Erotically rub the lips with the tender bits of fruit. Tease him or her with the bites afterward. Continue in your own imaginative way.

Erotic Dance

Have you ever seen a belly dancer rotate her hips from front to back and to the side? Was it erotic? You bet! Dancing to release and free the pelvis is fun to do. You can dance by yourself or with a partner. You can even make this an erotic dance if you choose.

Striptease

Perform a striptease for each other. Dress up in the sexiest clothes you have. Layer your undergarments so you have lots to take off. Then slowly take them off. When you're down to almost nothing, use a scarf or a sarong to do an erotic dance for your partner.

Here are a few exercises to help you release body tension and get comfortable for the erotic dance:

- Start by slightly bending your knees to protect your back. Place your feet about hip distance apart. Stick your bottom out and then gently thrust it forward. As you move your hips back, your neck and head move forward. Move slowly and easily at first. See if you can create a kind of "wave" to your body movement. Try to keep your torso fairly stable over your legs.
- Rotating your hips around in circles is great for your lower back and keeps the pelvis free and loose. Start with your hands on your hips so that you get a better feel of what is happening at the waistline. Keep it easy at first and go in both directions.
- Isolate your upper torso from your hips and legs. This is a classic belly dance practice. As you are doing the hip rotations, try holding your arms out to the side, in the air, and concentrate on moving your hips out and around but not your torso.
- Start by doing the pelvic rock. After you warm up with a few of them, stop while your bottom is thrust back and move your shoulders in first instead of your hips. If you follow through with the move, you'll feel a kind of a wave happen. Create a wave in your body and add your arms. They will naturally follow your hips once you get the basic wave.
- Move your arms around. As you dance, fling, stretch, wave, undulate, and make circles in the air with your arms. It's very good for blood flow and you'll strengthen them, too. Shake your hands vigorously to the beat of the music.
- Sing and just make noise if you feel comfortable doing it. Open up your vocal pipes. Make high-pitched sounds and then some low-pitched ones. Feel the difference in your body.

Adding a little lingerie to lovemaking can work magic. Women can try wearing a demi-bra or a pushup bra. Men can leave their silk shorts on or wear a muscle shirt to add excitement to lovemaking.

The key to a good, seductive erotic dance or striptease is to like what you are doing. If you slowly and seductively glance down at your own hip as it rotates and then look up into your lover's eyes, you are saying that you like what you see. It turns you on. Feast your eyes on your own body parts as you dance. That is the clincher when it comes to eroticism: Be turned on to yourself.

Chapter 5

Pleasure-Enhancing Practices

Though not strictly from the Kama Sutra, the more subtle arts of intimacy were part of daily routine in ancient India. These took the form of yoga, meditation, and rituals to honor the gods and goddesses. In this chapter, you'll learn about some of the pleasure-enhancing things you can do to increase the quality of your intimacy and orgasmic capacity.

Beyond the Kama Sutra

The Kama Sutra is great for explaining exotic positions, details of the physical and emotional types of men and women who exist, and how to make a good match for one's self. It covers how to make money as a courtesan, how a good wife should act and the things she should know, and how to handle the harem. However, it doesn't cover the fine details that Western sexologists, psychologists, and educators have discovered in more recent years.

The Fine Details

The Kama Sutra does not go into the exact sexual techniques that pertain to the teachings for modern society. Details on how to pleasure a woman's yoni are not extensive. It does say that the woman should be satisfied but doesn't say exactly *how*.

It's difficult to know the more subtle parts of the treatise as the translations, especially Sir Richard Burton's, can be somewhat inaccurate depending on the bias of the interpreter. Some of the other holy writings that occurred in the Hindu culture of the time covered more of the inner realm or subtle properties that one can bring to intimacy and sexuality, such as yoga, meditation, an understanding of breath, and healthful living strategies.

Modern scientists, sexologists, and educators know that these fine details are very important to the experience of great sex. You'll find hints and tips throughout this book that give you much more detail than the original Kama Sutra. Remember, that was the prerogative of the teacher of the Kama Sutra—to add the fine details.

Breath

Breath is the essence of life. It is something our bodies do without us thinking about it. If you have ever choked, had the wind knocked out of you, or gasped during a strenuous sports activity, you are aware that your breath is more precious than you had perhaps thought. If you ever take a beginning meditation class, the instructor will definitely point out the importance of the breath.

Types of Breathing

Many people have not been instructed in the proper way to breathe, which can be more life enhancing. We are taught to suck in our tummies and wear tight clothing, including belts and corsets. This forces us to breathe shallowly into our chests rather than into our bellies. The results are that we never get a full, luxurious breath of air.

Researchers know that the way you breathe has a tremendous impact on your life. Fast chest breathing induces panic and distress while slow, deep belly breathing creates bonding, emotional stability, and longer life. They have also identified a few men and women who can simply breathe their way to orgasm.

On the other end of the spectrum, belly breathing is grounding and stabilizing. Conversely, high-chest breathing is the type that is normally associated with the "fight or flight" phenomenon when we are frightened or anxious. This kind of breathing perpetuates itself because it causes hormones, such as adrenaline, to seep into our systems and cause anxiety. Relearning how to breathe is one of the most important things you can do to enhance your sexual experience and your life.

Deep belly breathing will expand your capacity to have more powerful orgasms. When you breathe deeply and relax, it isn't possible to tighten the pelvic muscles. This leads to a more orgasmic response capability.

Breath also plays a major role in premature ejaculation. For men, slow, deep belly breaths are key to staying relaxed in high states of arousal. This helps prevent premature ejaculation and is the key to moving into the multiorgasmic state.

The Basics of Deep Breathing

Deep breathing fills the abdomen first and then fills the chest cavity. The capacity of the lungs becomes larger when you fill the lower area of the lungs first and then the upper area. As a result, the breath will begin to slow down because there is more oxygen in the lungs to extend the breath. These are the basic steps:

1. Lie down on any firm surface—the floor or your bed if it's fairly firm. After you learn the techniques, it doesn't matter where you are, but for now make it a firm surface.
2. Remove any restrictive clothing, such as tight waistbands or belts.
3. Close your eyes for a moment and breathe. Notice how you breathe. Where is your breath, in your chest or in your belly?
4. Place one hand on your stomach, below your navel.
5. Begin to breathe into the hand that is on your belly. Push it up on the *in* breath and let it fall on the *out* breath. Exaggerate this movement.
6. Slow it down and let the hand rise and fall.

Perform at least ten of these breaths the first time and then work up to thirty. For best results, try to remember to do this practice twenty times a day. Bring deep breathing into your consciousness as many times a day as you can. Come back to the breath as you would during meditation.

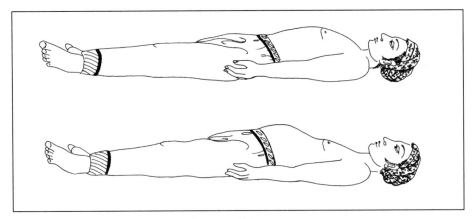

▲ Deep belly breathing

Feeling More Sexual Energy

Eventually you will breathe this way all the time, though it will take you some time to get to that place. Put little Post-it notes on your car's steering wheel, on your computer screen, at the kitchen sink, by your bed, and any other place that might be easy to notice them. It's especially great to put reminders at locations where you may most get triggered to move into anxiety, anger, or frustration. These are the places you will need calming breath the most.

A Quickening Breath for Women

Women do tend to take longer than men to reach the orgasmic plateau stage during sexual intimacy. It's helpful to know a few tricks to get yourself aroused quicker and stay in that zone for longer periods of time. Building your sexual charge higher is an art that is well worth striving for.

Deep breathing opens up the body cavity to more feeling. It allows the orgasmic pulses and pleasure to move through the body instead of being focused locally in the immediate genital area. The direct results are longer, more powerful orgasms, more pleasure, and much less tension.

Women who know how to raise their sexual turn-on more quickly have a greater capacity for learning and expanding even further. Try this exercise by yourself the first few times. It's an exercise in breathing and visualizing so, again, choose a quiet place with privacy.

1. Lie on the floor or bed on your back.
2. Close your eyes and deep-breathe into your belly for a few big breaths.
3. Now begin to quicken your breath. Breathe through your mouth but keep the breath in your belly, not the chest.
4. Do ten or twelve breaths like that, then go back to a few deep breaths.
5. Repeat the fast breaths, but at the end of the twelve (or so) breaths, purse your lips and slowly force the air out through your lips. Visualize your breath bathing the front of your body.

6. Now locate your clitoris or your G-spot in your mind. You can pump your PC (pubococcygeus) muscles a couple of times to locate one of them. Focus on it and feel it with your mind. You are not touching yourself at all.

7. Repeat the rapid breaths and visualize your clitoris or G-spot as you do them. You can even pump your PC muscles.

8. Repeat a series of ten breaths, three times. Relax when you are done for five minutes, breathing deeply but at a normal pace.

How did this feel? Did you start to hyperventilate at any time? If you did, then slow down and take several deep breaths between the sets of fast ones. Did you feel aroused at any time? The next time you practice this exercise notice your arousal levels. Start playing with this edge to increase your orgasmic capacity.

FACT

The recommendation of exhaling slowly, through pursed lips, might come in handy for extending the period of time you feel your orgasm. This is true for both men and women. Try this some time.

This exercise is also beneficial to men. You won't want to use it during sex unless you are having a hard time being aroused. If you don't have a problem in that area, be careful with this practice because it can cause you to get too excited, too rapidly.

Relaxation

Most of us in the modern world lead very stressful lives and have hardly any time to relax.

We rush to school or work, then back home. We cook, clean, spend time with our families, get some exercise, pay the bills, and start all over again the next day. But knowing how to relax is the key to a healthy life—and a good sex life.

Relaxation means a complete shutdown of the systems that keep us alert and on the go. Silence, privacy, soft music, a deep massage, a soft place to lie down, eye gazing with your partner as you lie close together on the bed—all these are deeply relaxing. You need relaxation to keep you emotionally stable and happy.

The Relaxation Exercise

Try this easy exercise. Lie down on the floor in a comfortable position. Place your hands at your sides and take a few deep breaths. Now tense your whole body for just a second or two. Let it go—and this time really let go. You can try a big sigh with your out breath to help. Tense again and then let go.

Do you notice the difference? You may have thought that you were relaxed when you started, but when you contrast it to tensing your muscles and then letting go, you can feel the difference. Once you find this deep state of relaxation, fall into it deeper for five or ten minutes. Close your mind and let the world go for just a little while. Your body and psyche will love you for it.

Eye Gazing

Eye gazing is something you may not be used to. In this culture, it's often difficult to meet someone else's eyes. You avoid each other's eyes because you feel that you have to protect yourself. Sometimes being vulnerable with a person you have just met isn't safe.

◀ Eye gazing—a stone sculpture from India

Be Seen

You can get out of practice at meeting another's eyes. This can even extend to your partners and lovers if you feel as though there is something you can't say to them. Being open and vulnerable with your lover means the lights have to be on—or at least a candle is lit. You must "be seen" and be able to "see" your partner.

ALERT!

When eye gazing, you should not try to do anything. Just relax. You won't need a smile on your face or a frown or a quizzical look. Just think about being open and soft and receptive. That's all it takes.

The Eye-Gazing Exercise

Sit facing your partner cross-legged or in two straight-backed chairs that are very close together. Your knees should be touching either way with your hands resting easy in your lap. Take a few deep breaths with your eyes closed to get relaxed. Open your eyes slowly and look into the eyes across from you. Nothing to do—nowhere to go—just gaze softly.

You may find that you want to giggle at first, or talk, or say that this is silly. Resist the temptation to giggle. Gaze into the eyes in front of you and see them as deep pools. Keep your eyes focused on your partner's for at least five minutes.

How did that feel? Did you find yourself dropping into your lover's eyes even deeper? Try eye gazing up-close next time, say, five inches from his face. How does that feel?

What's in It for You?

Eye gazing opens your soul to another. You have a chance to drop your defenses and practice being vulnerable. When you are physically close to someone you love, the chemicals of love get transmitted more readily.

Pheromones, the attraction chemicals your body produces, are transmitted via your breath. Oxytocin, the bonding chemical produced during lovemaking, orgasm, and childbirth, builds up when you gaze lovingly with your mate. Oxytocin improves your immune system, calms your breathing, and lowers your blood pressure. Those are all valuable components for a healthy lifestyle and they're produced by love and connection.

Building Sexual Energy

This technique is designed to heighten the sexual energy between you and your partner, as well as to expand your personal capacity for increased pleasure. You, like most of us, were probably taught to dummy-down your capacity for extended pleasure. Re-learning how to receive pleasure, build upon it, and spread the sensual and sexual energy you are being given takes practice.

Spread and Receive Sexual Energy

In this exercise, each partner will take about a twenty-minute turn and then switch until both partners have had a turn. You can actually continue this erotic exercise for as many turns as you'd like. It's also an exquisite way to start your lovemaking any time you feel in the mood to tease and be playful. The woman should be the first to receive.

FACT

The brain chemical category of endorphins produces comfortable attachment to family and partners; oxytocin produces bonding and physical intimacy; and dopamine, PEA, and norepinephrine cause us to feel excited and "high" on attraction and expectancy.

Arouse her sexually for three to four minutes in whatever manor the two of you choose. Encourage deep breathing and relaxation. Then, using both of your hands gently spread the energy up the body, away from the genitals, with four or five light strokes of the hand.

Instruct the receiver to take the energy you are sweeping over her into her upper body, along the spine and chest. Then, start the whole experience over again and continue until you have gone through four waves of building and spreading. You can now switch partners and repeat the exercise.

ALERT!

Ask yourself what is your uppermost capacity for receiving love and pleasure? With the practices in this book, you'll begin to transform the amount of pleasure you can receive. As a result, you'll expand the pleasure you give to others, too.

Use this technique during foreplay to arouse and tease your lover. It will enable the two of you to learn automatically how to expand the sexual feelings throughout your body every time you have sex. This will open the gateway to expanding your capacity to receive more pleasure. As can be imagined, this practice can be done solo, too. It is one of the components to learning the mastery of ejaculation for men.

Thrusting Patterns

Great lovers have learned that it isn't just about in and out, when it comes to making love. Men, how you go about the act of intercourse, once you are inside your partner, can play an important part in how both of you experience pleasure. Whole new dimensions can be added to lovemaking by being creative with thrusting techniques.

You can create a dance of churning, deep thrusting, then shallow thrusting, and then reverse the dance. Spend some time teasing by staying shallow during intercourse. Then, surprise your partner with some deep thrusts and a new set of techniques.

A Classic Thrusting Technique

A classic pattern of thrusting, suggested by one of the ancient erotic books, is nine deep thrusts, then one shallow (and slow) and eight deep thrusts, then two shallow and seven deep thrusts, and so on. This thrusting pattern allows the man to get very excited and then transfer that excitement to the woman. Varying the way a man thrusts will help him gain mastery over his ejaculation, too. He will be able to sustain intercourse longer if he learns to ride the energy of the union in this way.

Go slowly, eye gaze, and take deep breaths into your bellies. The breath carries the intense feelings throughout your body. It translates the acceptance of the pleasure to your brain.

Shallow thrusting stimulates the G-spot area more effectively. Generally, a woman will like deep thrusting and shallow thrusting at different times during arousal. Ask your partner what she likes best. Try making up your own patterns with the help of your partner.

Yummy Things to Do

Here are a few suggestions for some yummy additions to your oral pleasures. Let these be a starting point for you and your lover. Experiment and explore with each other.

- Eat dessert from your lover's body; whipped cream, chocolate and raspberry sauces, and mango are great.
- During oral sex on the man, try putting a small bit of any kind of liqueur in your mouth first before you start. This can have a warming effect that is quite sensational.
- Put something slippery and tasty on your lips before kissing or giving oral sex: lipstick or olive oil will work. Men can do this for oral sex on the woman, too, just remember that sugar and vaginas don't mix.
- Don't forget to use your hands when kissing or during oral sex. Put some wonderful lubricant or olive oil on and pleasure your lover with your hands as well as your mouth.
- Edible body paints are available from adult stores that are fun to use to express the latent artist in you. Put them on and then lick them off.

Create a fun environment that makes everything you do okay, and that passes no judgment on an idea or action. You may want to take turns at this. Each of you could take a half hour apiece to be the leader in discovering new ways to use your mouth erotically to make love to your partner.

Chapter 6

The Art of
Erotic Touch

There is no better way to express love than through the art of touch. Touch is a human need and the art of sensual touching is a skill to be developed. The Kama Sutra describes many variations on the quality of erotic touch, the type of caress appropriate to the moment, and the passionate qualities associated with certain types of touch. It is a science unto itself.

Showing Love Through Touch

The Kama Sutra offers very explicit and detailed information about passionate embraces, kissing, scratching, biting, shrieks and cries, and even striking blows (in certain ways and in certain areas of the body). While most amorous people will use these methods during lovemaking, some of the techniques are beyond what modern lovers feel are appropriate for them. With the additions of massage, conscious touching techniques, and knowledge of the body's erogenous areas, you will have the tools to develop your own erotic touch style.

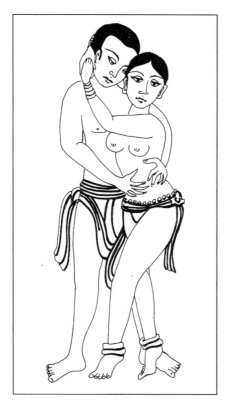

◀ Erotic touch is an art form.

Knowing Your Body

An understanding of your body, as well as your lover's, is immensely helpful when touching. Tender areas need to be loved in ways that don't cause your partner to react unfavorably by flinching or creating other disagreeable responses. Knowing your own erotic trigger areas and even developing new ones will add to your sensual experience. Once you know more about yourself, you can begin to expand that knowledge to its greatest potential.

Some people are good receivers and some are better at giving. It is a rare and fortunate person who is good at both. Cultivating both qualities will give you greater pleasure in your relationship.

There are three areas of nerve distribution on the body, and each corresponds to an amount of body hair and its distribution patterns. Basically, the more hair over an area of the body the fewer nerve endings per square inch that area will have. That does not mean, though, that those areas with fewer nerve endings are going to be less responsive to touch. It just means that they will respond differently. The areas are:

- **Tertiary:** These are the areas that have the more dense amounts of hair, such as the pubic triangle, the armpits, and the head.
- **Secondary:** These areas comprise most of the body and are covered with light, sparse hair. The secondary areas include the arms, the legs, the neck, the back of the hands, the back and chest areas, the buttocks, and the inside of the thighs.
- **Primary:** This category is the genitals, the anus, the erect part of the nipples, the mouth, and any area where hair is absent.

Everyone is aware of the feelings generated in the genitals to erotic touch, but you may not think about your arms or legs as being sensual. Though the hair is generally thick on the pubic triangle—and thus has relatively few nerve endings—it is one of the more erotic places. By gently pulling and teasing this hair during sex, you can highly eroticize the pubic area.

Most people love when their head is massaged and rubbed. It is erotically pleasing to have your hair pulled, scratched, and scrunched by a lover. The nerve endings in the scalp and the pubic area are near enough to the buried hair follicles in the region to transfer the stimulated feelings.

FACT

Sensual and sexual massage is a healthy pastime. The body is filled with lymph nodes, blood vessels, muscles, and vital organs that need stimulation to stay healthy. Massage is an erotic pastime that will always be received lovingly from your partner.

The same is true for scratching, biting, and even firm sucking. You would probably love to have your back, head, or arms scratched during sex but probably not your vaginal lips. This would hurt and not be appropriate because of the extra amount of nerve endings in this area. Love bites, sucking, and scratching should be placed in suitable regions on the body.

Training Your Mind and Body

Each and every one of these areas of the body is erotic to the touch, especially if you have trained your mind to feel it. A wonderful feedback loop can be created through conscious practice to connect any area of the body to sensational feeling. By stimulating the genitals in the ways you like best and stimulating another area of your choice, you can create both mind and body excitement to this new area.

Like a yogi, who can slow his breathing down to practically nothing, the body can be trained with practice and time to recognize a vast variety of stimuli and touch. It is in this way that you can truly give and receive the highest pleasure possible through touch. The first step is to bring your conscious mind to the task with your willing body.

It is known that some women can orgasm through nipple or other body part stimulation alone, without genital touching. These women have trained themselves to feel sexual in distinct areas of their bodies. There are also women, who can have orgasms by simply breathing a certain way. They have trained their bodies to respond in ways that the scientific world is just beginning to understand.

Other Forms of Touch

Touching doesn't necessarily mean just touching with hands and physical body parts. You might consider that a sensual gaze or an erotic stare might be a type of touch. It touches your soul. Loving words, erotic speaking, eye gazing, flirting with the eyes alone, dancing erotically for your partner—all of these things can be "touching." Sitting opposite each other and breathing in different ways while focusing on each other's eyes is a soul touch that can be very erotic to the practiced couple. Try dancing sometime to erotic music, such as belly dance or Middle Eastern music, keeping your eyes connected the whole time. Sway, seduce, and tease your partner while dancing. See how it "touches" you.

FACT

It is reported that the clitoris has approximately 8,000 nerves, all ending at its tip. That's twice as many as the penis has and many more than any other area of the body. It's no wonder the genitals are so sensitive to touch.

Erogenous Areas of the Body

Much has been written and discussed about erogenous zones. These areas of the body seem to be more highly erotic and sensitive than others. The amount of nerve endings in certain areas tends to distinguish parts of the body that are more easily used to help arouse an individual. Getting to know your areas and then developing a few new ones is great fun and can be very easily incorporated into love-play.

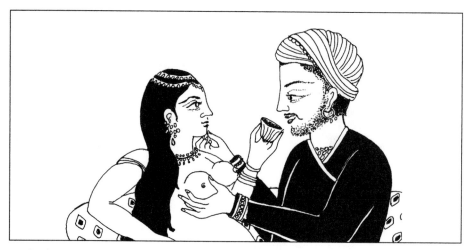

▲ The breasts are an erogenous zone.

It is obvious that the genitals are the first regions that come to mind when you think of erogenous zones. In most people, when even slightly touched, the genitals react immediately with warmth, then a change of color, and then swelling. No other body parts act like that with such little coaxing.

Not much conscious attention is put to the other areas of eroticism in the body, though. You may forget to try stimulating some of the other areas during lovemaking, but in doing so you ignore some potentially powerful additives to the sensual experience. Here are some areas you may or may not have thought about before:

- Breasts, under the breasts, nipples, and underarms
- Toes, in between the toes, and feet
- Buttocks, anus, and perineum
- Inner and outer thighs
- Neck areas, ears, and face
- Eyelids
- Love handles and sides of the torso from the underarms to the hips
- Backs of the knees and inside the elbows
- Fingers, in between the fingers, and wrists
- The back and the head

The Key to Great Touch

Following this deceptively simple rule will give you the key to great touch: The hand that is giving the touch should feel just as good (or better) than the body part receiving the touch. In other words, the "giver" should be in pleasure along with the "receiver." Think about this—it's quite a concept. The next time you give pleasurable touch to a person, think about your fingertips. Are they enjoying themselves? How could they be enjoying this experience even more?

As the "giver," you will find that you can really enjoy this role. You'll find new ways to touch that will open up the experience for both of you. This simple practice will transform sensual touch for you. It even works when the "giver" and the "receiver" is the same person. Try it. Above all, this is fun, so be light and playful.

As the "receiver," you should concentrate on the touch you are receiving. Breathe into the quality of the touch to such a degree that your "giver" can actually feel you receiving. Don't be afraid to make yummy sounds as a form of communication, too.

The key to fabulous touch is to remember that the fingers of the "giver" should feel just as good or better than the body parts of the "receiver." This ensures that both of you are having a great time.

The Blindfold Game

This is a great way to practice giving and receiving wonderful touch. You can improve your ability to give and receive each time you play and have a lot of fun, too. Take turns playing each role, possibly on different nights so that each of you really gets to honor and participate fully in the role you take. Set this game up as a ritual that will last for an evening.

Prepare the bedchamber with soft lights, candles, some incense, drinks, and anything else that you may need to be comfortable. You'll also need a blindfold of some sort. Gather a piece of velvet, a few rose petals, a soft makeup brush, the fresh end of a bamboo frond, a fringed scarf, a piece of fur, chocolate sauce, ice cubes, and anything else you can think of that might produce a sensual, erotic, but different kind of a feel. You may want to have some good-quality massage oil on hand, too, for a massage at the end of your exploration game.

Decide who will go first, then blindfold the person receiving and lay him or her down. As you treat the "receiver" to the sensual experience see if he or she can tell what you are using. Try the different modalities on different parts of the body, seeing which areas are more sensitive than others. Remember the varying dynamics of the erogenous zones and use this knowledge to its fullest potential.

ALERT!

You should encourage your partner to breathe deeply and relax. Encourage him or her to give you feedback and to make sounds of pleasure that he or she is feeling. Encourage and delight all the senses you can possibly bring into this love session.

The Sensual Bath

The sensual bath is another way to honor touch as an art form and to practice giving quality touch. You can either take the bath together or separately, but remember that the point is to give and receive the best touch possible. Create the sensual setting by using candles, music, scents, and even rose petals in the bath water.

Wash your lover's feet lovingly. Massage his shoulders while he reclines. Give him sips of fruit juice or wine. Present him with a warmed towel upon emerging from the bath. Gently towel dry him, and anoint him with a light oil or lotion when he is dry. Brush his hair thoroughly and sensually. Tell him that you love him and repeat it often. Now, switch places—it's your turn.

▲ The art of the bath

The Bath in Ancient India

The bath was an important part of the day's ritual during the time of the Kama Sutra. Great attention was given to the skin, teeth, hair, and general body. The hands and feet of women were often perfumed and painted with henna designs. Men shaved and shampooed every second or third day, but bathed (or dipped into water) every day. They also used limited amounts of perfumes. The Kama Sutra makes reference to cleansing the armpits and oiling the body every other day, as well.

Women, especially in the harems, bathed together. Along with handmaidens, they helped each other bathe, shampoo, brush and braid their hair, dress, paint henna, and embellish their bodies. It was a time of social interaction, too. Water has always held an important part in the culture of India. It is revered and thought to be holy.

Embracing

Many Westerners don't stop to think too much about the kinds of embracing they do, let alone give them names. However, this is the kind of thing you see in the Kama Sutra, and it contributes to the impression that sexuality comes down to a science for that culture. The names seem old-fashioned, but the actions are entirely recognizable today. Here are the four types of embraces detailed in the Kama Sutra:

1. Touching
2. Rubbing
3. Piercing
4. Pressing

Every inch of your skin is erogenous. Your skin has many thousands of nerve endings so let your imagination run wild. Be respectful of your partner and his or her likes or dislikes. Remember to ask permission to touch an area you think might be risky or extra sensitive.

Touching Embrace

"When a man under some pretext or other goes in front or alongside of a woman and touches her body with his own, it is called the Touching Embrace" (Part 2, Chapter 2, Sutra 9). When two people don't know each other (or don't know each other well) but seem enthralled by each other, they may create a situation so that they can touch. You've probably done it or at least thought about it at some point in your life. The titillation of just touching the person probably sent a rush of adrenaline through your body and made you long for more.

Very young boys and girls do this kind of thing to test the other person. It looks like teasing at a young age or even rough-housing, but it is that first spark of sexual interest rearing its head. When young adults do it, they are getting practice at just being in the presence of another person.

Piercing Embrace

"When a woman in a lonely place bends down, as if to pick up something, and pierces, as it were, a man sitting or standing, with her breasts, and the man, in turn, may grab her and hold her, it is called a Piercing Embrace" (Part 2, Chapter 2, Sutra 10). This embrace seems very bold on the part of the young man. It is a teasing kind of maneuver that has the girl wanting the kind of attention that she gets. "The above two kinds of embrace take place only between persons who do not, as yet, speak freely with each other" (Part 2, Chapter 2, Sutra 11).

Rubbing Embrace

"When two lovers are walking slowly together, either in the dark, or in a place of public resort, or in a lonely place, and rub their bodies against each other, it is called a Rubbing Embrace" (Part 2, Chapter 2, Sutra 12). Getting as close as possible is always good. With this embrace, you can pass pheromones through your breath and convey sexual innuendos in your body language.

Pressing Embrace

"When on the above occasion one of them presses the other's body forcibly against a wall or pillar, it is called a Pressing Embrace" (Part 2, Chapter 2, Sutra 13). By pressing or pinning, the couple is creating a private space where they can get closer and have their bodies rubbing more intentionally on each other.

"At the time of the meeting the four following kinds of embrace can be used: The Twining of a Creeper, the Climbing a Tree, the Mixture of Sesame Seed with Rice, and the Milk and Water Embrace" (Part 2, Chapter 2, Sutras 15–20). If a couple had an attraction to each other and was possibly already betrothed, these four different kinds of embraces were used along with the Pressing Embrace to show the degree of sexual turn-on the couple had for each other. Each gets hotter than the other before it.

This is the kind of information the Indian society of the day taught the young people so that they could be straightforward in their selection of a life partner. They were not beating around the bush when training young lovers.

Scratching and Marking

Scratching during sexual arousal and intercourse occurs when the partners are very turned on and passionate. It is very common for the passions to run high, and scratching your lover can help increase the passion. The Kama Sutra has very specific techniques for scratching and marking during sexual encounters. They go beyond what most Westerners might experience but are titillating nevertheless.

"When love becomes intense, pressing with the nails or scratching the body with them is practiced, and it is done on the following occasions: on the first visit; at the time of setting out on a journey; on the return from a journey; at the time when an angry lover is reconciled; and lastly when the woman is intoxicated." —Part 2, Chapter 4, Sutra 2

The most notable thing about this sutra is that the lover about to embark on a journey marks his or her partner with a nail mark that hurts and that lasts. The hurt is to remind the lover of what is left of the passionate moment shared. It is also to show others that their passion is strong.

"But pressing with the nails is not a usual thing except with those who are intensely passionate, i.e. full of passion. It is employed, together with biting, by those to whom the practice is agreeable. Pressing with the nails is of the eight following kinds, according to the forms of the marks that are produced: sounding or limited pressure; half moon or crescent moon shaped; a circular mark or full moon; a straight line; a tiger's nail or claw; a peacock's foot or a five-finger press; the jump of a hare or the marks of the peacock made close to one another on the breast presses; the leaf or petal of a blue lotus. The places that are to be pressed with the nails are as follows: the arm pit, the throat, the breasts, the lips, the pelvis, or middle parts of the body, and the thighs. But there is the opinion that when the impetuosity of passion is excessive, the places need not be considered." —Part 2, Chapter 4, Sutras 3–6

The Kama Sutra goes on to describe exactly what kinds of nail marks are left on what parts of the body and for what occasions. It is very precise and the marks are highly regarded by both the individual wearing the mark and those who see them upon their bodies. Marks that are left in private places remind the wearer of the erotic moment and of their lover.

"The qualities of good nails are that they should be bright, well set, clean, entire, convex, soft, and glossy in appearance" (Part 2, Chapter 4, Sutra 8). It further says that those with intense passion should file their nails on their left hand in two or three points like the teeth of a saw. Those with a medium passion should file their nails with pointed ends like the beak of a parrot, and those with mild passion should just slightly round their fingernails so that they will produce a crescent shape.

FACT

A recent survey of 2,400 respondents conducted by tantra.com, found that only 5 percent focused exclusively on themselves during sex. Thirty-nine percent focused primarily on their partner's enjoyment, and 55 percent said they focused on both equally.

Biting and Erotic Blows

Love bites are similar to nail marks in that they leave the wearer with a remembrance of the erotic activity that produced them. Nail marks, bites, and blows are all a little difficult to comprehend unless you are of a passionate nature and in the moment of pleasure that masks the intensity of the initial mark. Endorphins, chemical substances in your body that are enhanced when you are sexually excited and that cause euphoria, can mask any pain that occurs during the receiving of the marks. The reminder comes a bit later.

Biting Marks

There are eight kinds of biting marks that are described in the Kama Sutra, and they can be applied to various areas of the body. If a woman is resistant to a man making teeth marks on her but he doesn't stop, she must make even harder, deeper ones on him and in places where they will show to others. "When a man displays the marks made on his body by a woman and then points in her direction, she should simply smile to herself, unobserved by others. She should not be seen smiling even by the man, otherwise both will be considered rustic in manners" (Part 2, Chapter 5, Sutra 41).

Erotic Blows

"The union of the sexes, by nature, is a combat, offering plenty of scope for differences of opinion. In spite of its tender origin, such love leads to dizzy heights of intense passion, which, in its culmination, becomes blind to the force, and even the pain, of the ways and means used. Accordingly, in a state of high passion, striking or thrashing is considered one of the chief factors for arousing passion, the places most suitable for it being the shoulder, the head, the bosom, the back, the pelvis, and the sides" (Part 2, Chapter 7, Sutras 1, 2).

Erotic blows, or striking, during love-play are the ultimate in intense passion. The Kama Sutra illustrates the types of blows and the accompanying sounds that might be uttered.

Passionate Actions

In Kama Sutra, Vatsyayana claims that such passionate actions as scratching, marking, biting, and erotic blows, perhaps unacceptable or incomprehensible to some, are all part of the amorous play between lovers.

"Such passionate actions and amorous gesticulations or movements, which arise on the spur of the moment, and during sexual intercourse, cannot be defined, and are as irregular as dreams. A loving pair can become blind with passion in the heat of congress and go on with great impetuosity, paying not the least regard to excess. For this reason, one who is well acquainted with the science of love, and knowing his own

strength as also the tenderness, impetuosity, and strength of the young woman, should act accordingly. The various modes of enjoyment are not for all times or for all persons, but should be enjoyed at the proper times and in the proper places."
—Part 2, Chapter 7, Sutras 30–35

Vatsyayana further states that if a man and woman enjoy their lives and include variations in their lovemaking they will not fall out of love and may be partnered for 100 years. He likens lovemaking to eating. If you eat the same thing day in and day out, you will grow very tired of it, but if you stay creative and adventurous, you will thrive in your love-match.

The Art of Kissing and Oral Sex

Humans kiss for many different reasons throughout their lives. From a peck to a long, lingering seductive kiss, kisses are used for many varied encounters. Kissing can be the beginning of a sexual encounter or it can be a means to its own end. Whether you put lips to lips, or lips to other body parts, it is an art that can be expanded and refined over a lifetime.

The Nature of Our Mouths

Our mouths are exquisitely erotic though few of us stop to think about it. We take for granted the tender tissues, sensitive nerve endings, and the gymnastic capabilities of our tongues. We forget that even our food is sensuous and that eating (tasting) can be erotic. Along with the sense of smell, it is one of our senses that we take for granted when making love.

The ability to form words and have a developed language is uniquely human. That capacity has helped create a structure to our mouths that makes them very versatile. The muscles that control the tongue, lips, and whole mouth structure give us the ability to have great sensitivity and strength in that area. This all adds up to an exquisitely erotic organ that can serve you well in your lovemaking.

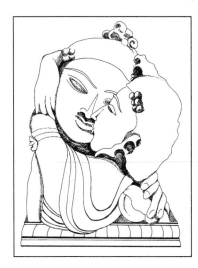

◀ Kissing is a great form of foreplay.

The Kiss

The pleasurable release of endorphins that accompanies deep, erotic kissing begins the flood of chemicals that readies you for sexual contact. When you are very close to someone and start kissing him or her, you come in contact with the odorless compounds of pheromones. Pheromones are the sexual attractants that draw us to each other. They are powerful chemicals that are produced in our sweat glands and other areas of our skin.

Spending an hour kissing with your partner is a rare treat that you may not think is "enough," but as a sensual activity it can really get you turned on. At other times, kissing is the prelude to other sexual activities that may lead to intercourse. This would include oral sex. Using your mouth to kiss and caress your lover's body all over is a very erotic experience. Kissing, licking, blowing warm air, and even light sucking on the neck, face, and other areas add to the sensuous arousal.

One time when kissing belongs is after climax when both of you may feel satiated. It is a bonding experience that should not be overlooked. Many women say that they miss this part at the end of lovemaking and wish their partners were more interested in it. It brings a sense of closeness, comfort, and closure to an otherwise wonderful experience.

The Treatise on Kissing

The *Treatise on Kissing* from the Kama Sutra covers the kinds of kisses you can use, the places on the body that the kisses should be placed, and the ways of kissing people who have never been kissed before. It also covers the arts relating to oral sex or oral kissing, as it's called in the Kama Sutra, for both men and women. It is descriptive in its detail and includes biting, scratching, and the order in which actions should occur. Vatsyayana concludes, very pragmatically, that when passion takes over there are no right or wrong ways to anything pertaining to lovemaking!

"It is said by some that there is no fixed time or order between the embrace, the kiss, and the pressing or scratching with the nails or fingers, but that all these things should be done generally before sexual union takes place, while striking and making the various sounds generally takes place at the time of the union. Vatsyayana, however, thinks that anything may take place at any time, for love does not care for time or order.

On the occasion of the first congress, kissing and the other things mentioned above should be done moderately, they should not be continued for a long time, and should be done alternately. On subsequent occasions, however, the reverse of all this may take place, and moderation will not be necessary, they may continue for a long time, and, for the purpose of kindling love, they may be all done at the same time." — Part 2, Chapter 3, Sutras 1–5

Places for Kissing

The Kama Sutra lists the places on the body that are most suitable for kissing. These places correspond to some of the primary and secondary erogenous zones spread out over the surface of the body. These are the forehead, the eyes, the cheeks, the throat, the bosom, the breasts, the lips, and the interior of the mouth.

FACT

Other suggested erogenous zones are the joints of the thighs, the arms, and the navel. It is well known that the inner thighs, the backs of the knees and elbows, and the sides of the torso are very sensitive.

Inexperience

There are three kinds of kisses to be practiced with inexperienced young women. They are the nominal kiss, the throbbing kiss, and the touching kiss. Here is how they are described:

1. "When a girl only touches the mouth of her lover with her own, but does not, herself, do anything it is called the 'nominal kiss'" (Part 2, Chapter 3, Sutra 10).
2. "When a girl, setting aside her bashfulness a little, wishes to touch the lip that is pressed into her mouth, and with that object moves her lower lip, but not the upper one, it is called the 'throbbing kiss'" (Part 2, Chapter 3, Sutra 11).
3. "When a girl touches her lover's lip with her tongue, and having shut her eyes, places her hands on those of her lover, it is called the 'touching kiss'"(Part 2, Chapter 3, Sutra 12).

It is obvious that the practices of ancient India allowed for the young, inexperienced person to lead the first encounters. Typically, even today, this is the woman and it appears as though she should lead by taking the next initiatives during the first kissing. Only she can take the experience deeper if she chooses. This is a wonderful acknowledgement of the idea that a sexual experience can only be so good unless both people are equally involved.

Four Kinds of Kisses

The Kama Sutra describes four main kinds of kisses, which get progressively more erotic and forceful. They are the straight kiss, the bent kiss, the turned kiss, and the pressed kiss. Try each of these in turn and find your own variations on them.

1. "The straight kiss results when simply the lips are in contact, facing each other" (Part 2, Chapter 3, Sutra 13-a).
2. "The slanting kiss requires one of the participants to slant the kissing lips diagonally against the other's lips" (Part 2, Chapter 3, Sutra 13-b).
3. "The turned is effected when one of the two lovers turns up the face of the other by holding the head and the chin, and then kisses" (Part 2, Chapter 3, Sutra 13-c).
4. "The pressed kiss takes place when any of the three varieties mentioned above is done with some force" (Part 2, Chapter 3, Sutra 13-d).

According to the Kama Sutra, these four kinds of kisses can also be done in two different ways: there is the pure kiss, when only the lips are used to do the kissing; and the tongue kiss, where the tips of the tongues come into play. So-called "French kissing" would call for the whole tongue to be used to investigate the far corners of the mouth. This might include the areas around the teeth, inside the lips, and the upper palate. The upper palate is very nerve sensitive and quite erotic. Usually deep tongue kissing comes a little later as the erotic charge and desire builds to it.

A Lesson in Kissing

Our lips are extremely sensitive and receptive to stimulation. Many people hold their lips rather stiffly, not allowing them to be relaxed and open to the receiving and giving required for good kissing. You might want to practice using your lips in more soft and open ways. Parting them slightly and keeping them moist gives an alluring appeal. This will also heighten their sensitivity.

Practice pouting softly when you are by yourself to relax the lips and expose more of the fleshy interior. In general, become more aware of your lips. Try eating your meals slower than you might usually, and really feel the food passing between your lips. You can practice sucking on soft fruit, such as a piece of mango or banana, for the sensual effect it has on your mouth and lips.

FACT

There is also a fifth kind of kiss that the Kama Sutra lists. "Holding the lower lip with the thumb and index finger, and shaping it to an 'O', and then kissing it with the lips only, without using the teeth" (Part 2, Chapter 3, Sutra 14). Try it.

When you are about to kiss, lick your lips to wet them, open your mouth a little way, tip your head very slightly, and go softly forward. Leave your tongue out of it for now. Gently explore the interior of your partner's lips with your lips. Move very slowly but with confidence. Go deeper, and open your mouth a bit more as you feel yourself moving into the kiss. Create a slight amount of suction as you expand and open your mouth a little bigger.

You can suck on the lower lip, the upper lip, and the corners of the lips. You can cover the same areas with light bites that include a little suction. Take your lover's whole mouth into yours. Do this lovingly, as if you are exploring it for the first time. Then, eat them up, but gently. Tease. Let them tease. The subtler you are with this, the better. Kissing can go on for a long time if it's treated playfully and erotically.

Love and pleasure—what is your capacity? If you're exploring the practices in this book, you'll begin to transform the amount of pleasure you can receive. As a result, you'll expand the pleasure you give to others, too. Remind yourself often that you can receive more pleasure.

The Art of Fellatio

The art of giving oral sex has come in and out of favor over the millennia—depending on which culture is being referenced. During the eras that the Kama Sutra was written, it was thought that oral sex was debasing, yet many people enjoyed it. The face was considered beautiful and morally "clean," and to have genitals touch it was considered wrong. Yet, it appears everyone was doing it!

Behave According to Your Inclinations

The Kama Sutra does go on to instruct in this fine art. Vatsayanya is liberal in his interpretation, saying: "Opinions differ on the matter of purity between the authority of the moral codes, occasional local customs, and one's own feelings. One should therefore behave according to one's inclinations" (Part 2, Chapter 9, Sutra 34).

It's curious to consider why there might have been restrictions during a time when generally the attitudes about sexual loving were quite liberal. Speculation on the subject might include that the contraction of illnesses and diseases was worrisome. It might also have been that by having only oral sex, a young woman of the times might get away with having unmarried sex yet, technically, still be a virgin.

Techniques for Kissing the Lingam

Fellatio is the term used for giving pleasure to the male's genitals with the mouth and tongue. Root words from the Latin include references to "swollen" and sucking. Here are the various techniques to consider when considering the art of fellatio:

- **Touching:** "When your lover catches your penis in her hand and, shaping her lips to an 'O', lays them lightly to its tip, moving her head in tiny circles, this is the first step" (Part 2, Chapter 9, Sutra 12).
- **Biting at the Sides:** "Next, grasping its head in her hand, she clamps her lips tightly about the shaft, first on one side then the other, taking great care that her teeth don't hurt you" (Part 2, Chapter 9, Sutra 13).
- **The Outer Pincers:** "Now she takes the head of your penis gently between her lips, by turns pressing, kissing it tenderly and pulling at its soft skin" (Part 2, Chapter 9, Sutra 14).
- **The Inner Pincers:** "Next she allows the head to slide completely into her mouth and presses the shaft firmly between her lips, holding a moment before pulling away" (Part 2, Chapter 9, Sutra 15).
- **Kissing:** "Taking your penis in her hand and making her lips very round, she presses fierce kisses along its whole length, sucking as she would at your lower lip" (Part 2, Chapter 9, Sutra 16).
- **Striking at the Tip:** "While kissing, she lets her tongue flick all over your penis and then, pointing it, strikes repeatedly at the sensitive glans and tip" (Part 2, Chapter 9, Sutra 17).
- **Sucking a Mango:** "Now, fired by passion, she takes your penis deep into her mouth, pulling upon it and sucking as vigorously as though she were stripping clean a mango seed" (Part 2, Chapter 9, Sutra 18).
- **Swallowed Whole:** "When she senses that your orgasm is imminent she swallows up the whole penis, sucking and working upon it with lips and tongue until you are spent" (Part 2, Chapter 9, Sutra 19).

Ejaculation Mastery

More will be said about ejaculation mastery in a later chapter, but it's important to add a note here. The giver usually controls the outcome of the oral sex experience when the man is receiving. More often than not the giver thinks that she is really good when she takes her lover over the top quickly. You are doing your lover and yourself an injustice if you do this.

ALERT!

Don't try to control the situation like that. Along with quick self-pleasuring, this is the way men get trained to go over the top too quickly. Train them to last a long time by "peaking" them, having them relax between peaks, and then repeating. Your man will quickly learn to last longer while you're both having fun!

Things to Remember

There's something mysterious and forbidden about oral sex, yet it's desirability cannot be denied. The control and surrender, the visual aspects for the couple, and the vulnerable nature of an act that has had a history of shame surrounding it are powerful motivators. It can often be a source of struggle for couples when one partner wants it and the other does not want to give it or get it.

When men voice their sexual fantasies and dreams, they often contain elements of oral sex. This has been true for so long that it's covered in the Kama Sutra and earlier texts, such as the Kama Shastra. When both partners really enjoy giving and receiving oral sex, it is an erotic and arousing addition to lovemaking.

Remember, confidence, not techniques, is the ultimate sensual driver. You can build confidence by knowing you are doing something that turns you on, and that you want to be doing it. It's nice to know techniques but wanting to explore, have fun, and pleasure your partner are the most important parts of this intimate journey.

The Act

Start by using your fingers to softly and tenderly brush the hair near and around, but not on, his "jewels" (the erotic adventurers of the past liked to call the genitals of both men and women by symbolic names). Gently tease, pull, and even nibble bits of the hair. You might try blowing your warm breath over the area. Move slowly but deliberately.

As you tease and excite him, place light kisses on his inner thighs, below his navel, and then zero in on the base of his penis. Work your way up to the head, placing kisses along the way. At this point, wet your lips and, as gently as you can, take the lingam into your mouth.

Notice the sensations in your upper palate. How does your mouth feel? Is it soft and wet? Are you thinking versus feeling your own pleasure? There is an energetic, and possibly physical, connection between the upper palate in the mouth and the G-spot in women. Really focus on how good this feels to your mouth and your partner is going to have a great time!

It's always very yummy to begin with a "soft-on." As you feel the lingam growing, you can create a little more suction with your mouth. Put attention on the feedback loop that is created between you, your sensations, and then his sensations—back and forth. Pay attention to this because, if you are new to this, it will help you enjoy the experience more.

There are as many variations on how to give oral sex as there are people to give it. Focus more on fun, exploration, and variety. Don't move too fast or make too many different moves in a short period of time. Use your hands at the same time you are using your mouth. You can add a variety of strokes like pulling down on his shaft while pulling up with your mouth, or cup and gently pull his scrotum as you pleasure him with your mouth.

The Art of Cunnilingus

During the time when the Kama Sutra was at its height in India, the "oral arts" were highly honored. Not many of the ancient pictures depicted the act, though, and even today it is much more common to see men being given oral sex than women.

Techniques for Kissing the Yoni

Cunnilingus is the term used for giving pleasure to the female's genitals with the mouth and tongue. It is derived from the ancient words *Cunti* and *Kunda*, or "womb of the Mother" and "womb of the universe." Many Asiatic cultures used descriptive metaphors to describe genitals and lovemaking acts. They might call the vagina (yoni) a "lotus," "jade palace," or "cinnabar gate." A man's penis (lingam) might be called a "wand of light," "jade stalk," or "jewel."

ALERT!

Cleanliness is next to godliness so bathe together as a start to your erotic activity. Lay your partner down gently and touch her body lightly all over. You may even want to begin with a light massage. This doesn't have to be long, but it really helps to get both sexes more present and in the mood.

The use of the word "seed" when referring to the woman means her love juices, as the people of ancient India likened the semen of the man to the juices of the woman. "Love-temple" is vagina and "archway" is referring to the lips of the labia and the hood that covers the clitoris. These are sweet endearments that show honor and a relationship to the sacred nature of the body. Here are some of the types of maneuvers that the Kama Sutra recommends for giving a woman oral sex. Notice some of the words that are used:

- **The Quivering Kiss:** "With delicate fingertips, pinch the arched lips of her house of love very, very slowly together, and kiss them as though you kissed her lower lip" (Part 2, Chapter 9, Sutra 31).
- **The Circling Tongue:** "Now spread, indeed cleave asunder, that archway with your nose and let your tongue gently probe her 'yoni' (vagina), with your nose, lips, and chin slowly circling" (Part 2, Chapter 9, Sutra 32).
- **The Tongue Massage:** "Let your tongue rest for a moment in the archway to the flower bowed Lord's temple before entering to worship vigorously, causing her seed to flow" (Part 2, Chapter 9, Sutra 33).
- **Sucked:** "Next, fasten your lips to hers and take deep kisses from this lovely one, your beloved, nibbling at her and sucking hard at her clitoris" (Part 2, Chapter 9, Sutra 37).
- **Sucked Up:** "Cup and lift her buttocks, let your tongue-tip probe her

navel, slither down to rotate skillfully in the archway of the love-god's dwelling and lap her love-water" (Part 2, Chapter 9, Sutra 38).

- **Stirring:** "Stirring the root of her thighs, which her own hands are gripping and holding widely apart, your fluted tongue drinks at her sacred spring" (Part 2, Chapter 9, Sutra 39).
- **Sucked Hard:** "Place your darling on a couch, set her feet to your shoulders, clasp her waist, suck hard and let your tongue stir her overflowing love-temple" (Part 2, Chapter 9, Sutra 40).

Helpful Pointers

Here are some important pointers to fully enjoy the art of oral sex. Give each other total permission to help the other get the most out of the experience. Begin your communication with a positive statement: "Honey, I like the way you are . . ." Then ask for a single, simple change: "Would you try moving your tongue a little to the left?" And, finally, "Thank you. That feels great," or "Yum." If it didn't work so well, then say that too. If you "sandwich" your request like this, you'll always get a positive response from your partner.

FACT

Approximately 80 percent of women indicate that the upper left area (2:00 on a clock if you are looking at her) is by far the most sensitive. Once you've discovered this, you'll have an easier time pleasuring her.

With your newfound communication skills, you can get down to the business of pleasure. Here is another fun and educational experience. Ask your lover if there is any location on her clitoris that feels better than any other place. Have her move her lubricated finger very slowly all the way around her clitoris.

The important thing about touch is that the giver's fingers and hands should feel better than the receiver's skin. Think about it: If what you are doing feels really good to you; then it's going to feel really good to your partner. Softly stroke your forearm right now. Try to make your fingers feel better than your arm. It takes focus to do this, but the outcome is fantastic. Use your hands when you are giving oral caresses by running them lightly over her thighs and soft hair.

FACT

It's important to note that more women can achieve the orgasmic state through oral sex and clitoral stimulation than through intercourse. A survey taken on the Web site tantra.com revealed that only 23 percent said they always have orgasms when having partnered sex.

Get some tip-of-your-tongue exercise first by playing with a "pea in a pod." Explore all around the pea with your tongue-tip. You can also flick your tongue over and behind your front teeth when you're driving or doing something where no one will notice. Focus your attention on the tip of your tongue to get the maximum out of your exercises.

The Act

Start by kissing her inner tights, stroking them lightly, and then move slowly inward, with focused attention. Use a more general kind of approach and then get specific. Women generally prefer to start slowly and build their passion as they go. Relaxation and trust are built this way, and so is her orgasmic response.

As you begin to kiss her vulva (the external genital organs of the female, including the labia, clitoris, and vestibule of the vagina) area, use your fingers to tenderly separate the lips of her labia. You can kiss and lick the outer and inner labia, slowly working your way to the clitoral hood and the clitoris. Use longer, sweeping strokes to begin with and shorter strokes when you get near her clitoris.

You may want to experiment with changing positions a few times while you are giving her oral kisses. Try having her lie on her back while you are on your hands and knees above one of her shoulders. If she reports that her clitoris is more sensitive on her left, then be on her left side. If it is the right, then be above her right shoulder. This allows you to pleasure the side of her clitoris that is the most sensitive with direct action from your tongue.

Women tend to like sustained, repetitive motions for a while and then a move of location and a slightly different stroke. Ask your partner what she likes, and then periodically, ask her if she likes what you are doing at a specific moment.

As she gets closer to the orgasmic zone, remind her to relax and breathe deeply into her belly. If she is tending to arch her back, that will give you more access to her clitoris. If she is tending to curl inward a little, you may be being too aggressive and a bit too firm in your touch. Back off a little and watch her response. The clitoris is very sensitive.

This is an interactive game you are playing. Trust your insight and intuition but ask for feedback, too. The better you get at both of these modalities of "knowing," the higher the two of you will go together. Ⓔ

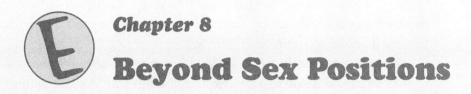

Chapter 8

Beyond Sex Positions

New positions are possibly the best way to introduce variety and interest into a sexual relationship. There are really only a handful of basic positions, but there are many variations on each of the basic ones, leading to greater pleasure for any couple. By learning and bringing to the experience the depth of all that is possible, you begin to truly open the door to a magical sexual relationship.

Asanas of the Kama Sutra

The Kama Sutra is often seen as the ultimate catalog of sexual *asanas* (Sanskrit for posture or positions). It's a good start, but there are also other love manuals with different positions and techniques that the Kama Sutra doesn't cover in detail. As you study this book, remember the basic categories and then explore the variations within each, rather than trying to remember 101 different positions. If something you read or see excites you, try it soon.

You can count on having new things to learn together when you investigate new positions. When exploring them with a sense of fun, they will lead to laughter, confusion, communication, and a sense of accomplishment. You'll probably find that some will work well for you, and some just won't work at all.

ALERT!

When trying a new position, take it slow at first and stay very conscious of your partner and his feelings. New positions can trigger long-buried emotions and feelings of vulnerability. Keep communication open, and be willing to stop and explore the feelings that are coming up for both of you.

One of the great discoveries about positions is that after you've tried a few new ones, much of your awkwardness or reluctance will disappear. You'll find yourself willing to try other new things with your lover. That's what makes exploring different techniques so important. Trying something new will often lead to a transformed sexual relationship.

Not only are new positions fun to try, they are also often the key for women to learn how to increase their pleasure and help create the possibility of vaginal or G-spot orgasms. Men will also get much more satisfaction from intercourse by discovering positions that increase their stamina and give them better control over how long they last.

The Great Variety of Positions

There are as many positions for sexual intercourse as there are possibilities in the creative mind. Having an open and adventurous mind will help you and your partner bring more playful energy into the quest for new, exciting sexual pursuits like exploring positions. Keep your spirit open to extraordinary possibilities and they will come.

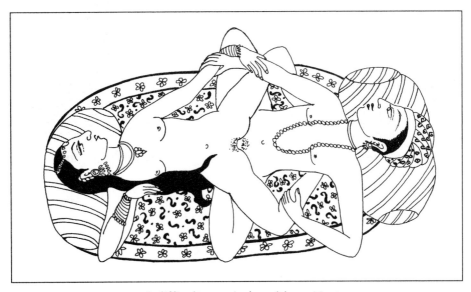

▲ A difficult, magical position—Yantra

Explorers of the Past

Love guides from India, China, Persia, Japan, Arabia, and even some of the North American Indian tribes have found their way into our modern culture. Many have a history of being secret societies and the teachings were only available to a few. It is a gift to have the wisdom of the scholars who put down these teachings in writing for us today.

A Subtle Shift Equals Perfection

There are many subtle variations on each major group of positions. Don't abandon a new position right away if it's not working for you. Ancient cultures that advanced lovemaking to an art form kept many props close by to help them. Have available pillows of varying sizes and shapes like crescent moons, rounds, and squares to use under heads, arms, legs, buttocks, tummies, and feet to subtly change angles and positions.

In the past, sexual asanas (positions) held a more important role than today. The ancients often thought of them as magical diagrams that lovers would arrange themselves in for spiritual transcendence. Besides yogic skills, conscious effort was put into forming the shapes and creating the experiences for extraordinary sexual intimacy.

Communication

When trying anything new, keep the communicating going. Say what you like and what doesn't work for you. Remember, very few of us are mind readers, and our partner may change his or her mind, anyway. So when in doubt, ask. If your partner is quieter than you are, encourage him to speak. Ask multiple-choice questions, such as, "Do you prefer that I do this faster or slower?" or "Do you like this harder or softer?" Even if the answer is "none of the above," just knowing that you care can give partners the courage to speak up.

Your Love Muscles

The pubococcygeus muscles, or PC muscles, are the pelvic floor muscles that hold your internal organs in place. They are the muscles you use to stop and start the flow of urine and bowel movements, or to push during childbirth. They are also part of the muscle groups that contract during an orgasm. Having strong, healthy PC muscles is an invaluable tool for having fabulous sex.

High headboards, love swings, and even the floor may all have their place in your lovemaking repertoire. Get creative and keep it fun!

Sexercises

Sexercises are exercises that get you in tiptop shape for sex. Sex can be exercise but when you tend to do it the same way every time, sexercises can give you a new frame of reference. Orgasms become stronger when the PC muscle groups are healthy and strong. These exercises help keep your bladder strong, your arousal levels up, and your sexual repertoire sophisticated.

This is the best set of exercises you'll ever learn. They are best known to help strengthen and tone the whole pelvic floor to prevent incontinence during middle and older age. If you keep your PC muscles in good shape, you will be better able to identify and distinguish your G-spot and anal muscles. As you perfect these exercises, you'll also begin to notice that you can isolate distinctly separate groups of muscles in your pelvic floor. This enables you to isolate your clitoris, for instance, and stimulate yourself at any time. It's an excellent trick for getting yourself "juiced up" for a hot date or romantic evening.

FACT

The Taoists knew that sexual exercises for men increased longevity, increased their sexual prowess, and kept their prostate gland in good health. In the past, these exercises were a part of many Asian men's daily health practices.

You may even be able to train yourself to have orgasms in this manner. The PC muscle exercises, known as Kegel exercises, increase blood flow to the pelvic region, which aids in the increased flow of hormones and helps engorge the vaginal area. With increased blood supply and stronger muscles, you'll be preparing yourself for better, stronger, and more amazing orgasms. Your G-spot is directly energized and stimulated when you are doing your Kegels.

Men will create stronger muscles for firmer erections and increase the angle at which their penis stands up by doing these exercises. In addition to obtaining amazing sexual prowess, a man's prostate and bladder will become much healthier. Mastery of these sexercises are the first step to improving ejaculation because they teach you to become much more aware of your pelvic floor in general and allow you to recognize how to relax completely. Relaxation is a key to ejaculation control mastery.

Kegels for Women

To begin your Kegel exercises, identify the muscle group you will be working by going into the bathroom and starting and stopping the flow of urine a few times. Make sure that you aren't mistaking the buttocks muscles for the pelvic muscles. Don't clinch your anus; just focus on your yoni area. Now, in a comfortable place to start, clinch and relax those same muscles. If this is new to you, you're not going to feel very good at it at first. Relax, breathe deeply into your belly, and focus—you'll get it. Breathe in with the clinch and out with the relax stage.

Do fifty of them at your first sitting if you can. You can roll up a small towel and sit on it the long way as you do these, though it's not necessary. It will apply slight pressure to help you feel what you are doing. Remember to relax fully between each clinch. This is very important. Go as slowly as you need to at first.

Over a period of several weeks, build up to 200 Kegel exercises a day. These should take about seven minutes and you can do them while driving or sitting at work. But, to start, do them in a quiet place so that you can really focus.

After a few weeks, you should be able to begin isolating your muscle groups. Start to feel this by focusing on your clitoris first. Squeeze as lightly as you can—right at your clitoris. Pulse a little. Now engage the next group and then the next. Don't be too discouraged if you can't feel it very strongly yet. It will happen, and you'll be amazed at the grip and power those forgotten muscles have.

There are devices available to help you get really good at these exercises. Eggs, barbells, and weights are recommended if you want to be an expert. You can even buy squeezing devices that have meters on them so that you can tell how much you are improving. These are generally recommended by doctors for women who are having a lot of trouble with incontinence.

Once a woman has gotten these exercises down, she can surprise her lover during lovemaking. Vary the sensations by exploring thrusting patterns that incorporate shallow and deep penetration along with gripping and letting go. If your partner is doing his set of sexercises, then begin to practice together in a position that both of you like.

Kegels for Men

Generally, men will follow the same instructions as women. Identify the PC (pubococcygeus) muscle group by starting and stopping the flow of urine a few times. Men can test their PC muscles by trying to use them to lift the erect penis. The higher you're able to lift your erection, the stronger your PC muscles actually are. Men, you will notice that you can "lift" your erection a little higher when you squeeze. However, you can do Kegel exercises when you don't have an erect penis.

To begin, clinch your pelvic muscles and relax consciously fifty times at one sitting. You can roll up a small towel and sit on it the long way as you do these, though it's not necessary. It will apply slight pressure to help you feel what you are doing. Remember to relax fully between each clinch and try not to squeeze your anus area. It's important to consciously try to separate the two.

Men vary in the angle of erection their penis has. Younger men tend to have angles that point upward. As men age, they tend to loose the upward swoop. This angle directly affects the G-spot in the woman. Kegel exercises can strengthen the muscles that control this arch.

Build up to 200 a day, over a period of several weeks. These should take you about seven minutes each time you do them. Some men even get to the stage of hanging weights on themselves. If you want to do this, start with a dry washcloth draped over your erection. Add weight to it later by wetting the corner.

It's important to remember to breathe deeply into your belly while doing these exercises. Breathe in with the clinch and out when you relax. Pay attention to your breath and you'll be actually meditating while doing your sexercises. Double duty!

Advanced Practice

When you have mastered 200 repetitions a day and feel like your muscles have caught up to the new exercise demands, you can add a set of sustained Kegels to your repertoire. When you first try these, you should probably be sitting in a chair with your feet on the ground.

- Begin by slowly tightening your PC muscles to the count of ten (or to whatever number you can get to when you're beginning).
- Hold and take one long, slow, deep belly breath and let that breath out without letting your muscles go.
- On the next in-breath, tighten one more time. You can also visualize at your third eye point if you are so inclined at this moment. Roll your eyes up slightly to "see" it (your third eye) and visualize anything you want to bring to higher consciousness.
- Begin to let that breath out slowly and let your muscles relax by gradually letting go. Do this in steps of ten if you can.
- Work up to twenty reps. You can put these into the middle or at the end of your 200 regular Kegels.

Pompoir and the Mare's Trick

Women throughout history have been known for their sexual tricks and abilities. Though many of these tricks are beyond what the modern woman might want to accomplish, they are nonetheless fun to know. You'll get partially good at them if you do your Kegel sexercises.

Pompoir, or Milking

The art of *pompoir,* or milking the penis, is a great technique to use with many different lovemaking positions. It's an art that the best courtesans were adept at, but many wives mastered it as well. Try it while practicing some of your favorite positions to see which ones it works best with. To perform this technique, contract your PC (pubococcygeus) muscles while the penis is inside you, simulating a "milking" action.

FACT

Placing your fingers in a circle or using a soft ring, made for this purpose, around the lower part of his penis will help keep the blood in longer. His erection will be stronger and he may last longer, too.

Here is how the "milking action" happens. When the PC muscles are in very good shape, they have the ability to ripple when they are squeezing. Because there are so many overlapping muscle groups in the pelvic area, the muscles can isolate themselves, and you can operate them in isolation, too. As you get better at your practices, you'll notice how effectively you can isolate those muscles.

This rippling effect also happens during an intense orgasm in a woman. The rippling causes a kind of milking action that starts at one end and moves along the vagina. This then translates to the action being felt by the penis, hence, the milking effect. *Pompoir* does take a while to perfect, but it is well worth it.

The Mare's Trick

The "Mare's Trick" is the ability to hold your lover's penis inside of you and not let it go. This is best accomplished in the "Clasping Position" or the "Twinning Position." The woman brings her legs tightly together while also tightening her vaginal muscles. If she is very good at it, the blood won't leak back out of her lover's penis and he won't get soft.

Thrusting Techniques

One thing great lovers have learned is that it isn't just about in and out during intercourse—it's about creating a kind of dance. Subtle moves, noticing what your partner responds to, and knowing some great tricks are what make lovemaking a treat. Varying your thrusting patterns, while you pay attention to your lover's pleasure clues, will turn you into a great lover.

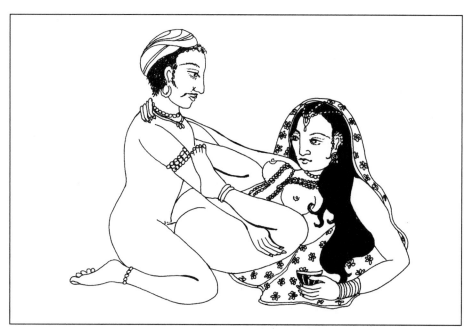

▲ A good position to practice thrusting techniques

Classic patterns for thrusting have come from some of the ancient Chinese erotic books. One pattern that is suggested is nine deep thrusts, then one shallow (and slow) and eight deep thrusts, then two shallow and seven deep thrusts, and so on. You increase one type as you decrease the other.

Shallow thrusting stimulates the G-spot area more effectively. Generally, a woman will like deep thrusting and shallow thrusting at different times during arousal. Ask your partner what she likes best. Try making up your own patterns with the help of your partner.

Go slowly, eye gaze, and take deep breaths into your bellies as you pay attention to the patterns. The breath carries the intense feelings throughout your body. It will expand and heighten the pleasure you are feeling and carry it throughout your body.

Try staying shallow and then surprise her with three deep thrusts. Create a dance of churning, deep thrusting, then shallow thrusting, and then reverse the dance. This is when the sexercises come in to use. They will build up your stamina and allow you to get very creative with your love moves.

Thrusting patterns also allow the man to get very excited and then transfer that excitement to the woman. Keeping track of where you are in the pattern will help you control your ejaculatory response levels, too. Don't get too lost in the act of keeping track, though. You'll get better at being able to focus both on what you are doing and the pleasure you are feeling as you practice these techniques more often.

Tips and Hints

Sexuality can be transformational so having a few "extra" hints to add to your practices and new techniques always helps to keep the learning and growth moving forward. As you take things a few steps deeper, your understanding will increase as well.

Breath

It will never be said enough—breathing is vitally important. Deep-breathe into your belly during all sexual activity. Use the faster breathing techniques outlined in Chapter 5 to enhance and build your sexual energy and response. With a little practice, you'll notice the difference in arousal and response.

ALERT!

During intercourse, and when thrusting, it's preferable for the penis and the vagina to stay in close contact. It can be dangerous, when going in and out, to pump air into the vagina.

Involve the Clitoris

In the Kama Sutra, Vatsyayana said that the female should be excited first by using the hand to stimulate her clitoris before the man enters her. Contrary to popular belief, there aren't really many positions that directly stimulate the woman's clitoris. Partners have to go out of their way to get the clitoris involved, but there are things you can do to stimulate this arousal area during lovemaking.

In positions where the two of you are lying very close together, try rubbing back and forth, head to toe, instead of thrusting. This action rubs the clitoris sufficiently to stimulate it to orgasm. The "Clasping Position" and the "Twinning Position" are great for this.

In the rear-entry positions, which are covered in Chapter 11, either the man or the woman can use their free hands to stimulate the clitoris. The woman can stimulate her own clitoris when she is in some of the female-superior positions. The male-superior position called the "Splitting of a Bamboo" also offers the opportunity to stimulate the woman's clitoris with the hands.

Visualize

Here's a Tantric exercise you can add to your Kegel practice if you choose to:

Add visualization to your Kegel exercises. It is a fine way to begin an introduction to meditation practice or advance an already existing one. Sit in a quiet place and begin your exercises. As you progress, hold a "picture" or thought in your mind that you have decided on before you began the exercise. It can be as simple as "love," or "gratitude," or the vision of "health" or "energy."

You can even take it as far as imagining light or energy passing up your body and out the top of your head. An even more advanced practitioner might imagine the energy going up her spine, out her head, and then recirculate it down the front of her body back to the genitals. This is how the Taoists recirculate the orgasmic energy to have it available to them throughout the day.

As you pump your muscles, you will also be pumping up your energy. You can also visualize your G-spot or your clitoris while doing these exercises. By doing so, you will have a mental picture of these two arousal areas and be able to better "visualize" them while making love. This will aid you in developing your orgasmic capacity.

Know Yourself and Don't Rush

Remember to only do what feels comfortable at any given moment. You can always come back to the exercise. Don't continue if you feel like you're going to hyperventilate, or cramp, or if you need a break. It will often take a little while to get into the flow. Be gentle with yourself. Have fun. If you are working with your partner, as you're experiencing the peaks, have him or her brush the energy up your chest, and away from your genitals.

Chapter 9

Woman-on-Top Positions

The Kama Sutra refers to woman-on-top positions as "woman assuming the man's role." It treats the subject with a delicious intrigue and obvious support. Though the chapter can be translated several ways, as you'll soon see, the underlying factor is apparent—when passion ignites, there is no stopping even a bashful girl. All is truly fair in love and war.

The Nature of an Erotic Woman

Empowering, satisfying, vulnerable, creative, and edgy—all these adjectives and more can be applied to positions where the woman is acting the role of the man—or "on top," in more modern terms. Sometimes women want to be "controlled" and sometimes they want to "control." Assuming the top position can have the effect of bringing out the powerful "animal passion" in any woman. It's a wonderful lover who will allow his woman her full repertoire of sexual expression.

A Historical Perspective

Many cultures of the past have kept women in a very subservient role. The relationship between men and women depended on the two having distinctly separate identities. Women were often accused of being in league with the devil when they showed tendencies toward powerful sexual urges—and even when those urges were with their husbands behind their own bedroom doors. Sexual energy was repressed in women.

The society at the time of the Kama Sutra honored a woman's sexual urges and honored courtesans as well. They were considered "wives of the city" and were respected by all. The idea that each man and woman also contained a balance of the other's energy pervaded the philosophy of the times. The principle of the yin/yang considers that every individual contains both male and female characteristics, and that these should be developed inside each of us as fully as possible.

ALERT!

Women can help their men last longer during sex. By playing the roll of the sexual initiator and encouraging position changes during lovemaking, you can slow things down for your man. Pay attention to his breath and movements to know when to initiate a shift in positions.

Role Reversal

Not only is the role of the woman acting as the man a fabulously fun thing to do while having sex, it allows the woman an expression she isn't often afforded in other ways in life. Being the leader in the sexual role means that the man must take a back seat for a while. Her energy is driving the experience and that means that he must give up control. This can be difficult for some men, but makes it all the more important as a life lesson.

It is often women themselves who hold back by keeping in line with social mores. It's difficult to overcome the training that our families, churches, communities, and cultures might have put us through. Personal fears often keep women from exploring a fuller range of possibility when it comes to sexuality.

If you haven't tried any of the "top positions," now is the time to try. Be gentle with yourself, and be sure to tell your partner of any vulnerable feelings you are experiencing.

"When a woman sees her lover is fatigued by constant congress, without having his or her desire satisfied, she should, with his permission, lay him down upon his back, and give him assistance by acting his part. She may also do this to satisfy the curiosity of her lover, or her own desire for novelty" (Part 2, Chapter 8, Sutra 1). The sutras say that the woman may either start the lovemaking this way or the couple may move into these positions in due course. However, she should take care not to let slip the man's lingam from the Love Temple. "She climbs upon you, the flowers dropping from her tousled hair, her giggles turning to gasps; every time she bends to kiss your lips her nipples pierce your chest" (Part 2, Chapter 8, Sutra 3).

All Is Fair in Love and War

The Kama Sutra actually encouraged women to be forceful in their passionate pursuits. It details when and how a woman might get back at her lover when she is angry or even pretending anger. Love was thought of as a sort of sport (or game) to be played and all was fair as long as no one got physically hurt. If feelings were hurt, they got mended before the love play was complete.

"As her hips begin to churn, her head, flung back, bobs ever faster; she scratches, pummels you with small fists, fastens her teeth in your neck, doing unto you what you have often done unto her" (Part 2, Chapter 8, Sutra 3). If her partner thought to put love marks on her, like bites and scratches, then she was encouraged to return the marks. "Though a woman may be reserved and try to hide her feelings and desires, she cannot successfully do so when she assumes the role of the man through intense passion" (Part 2, Chapter 8, Sutra 30).

Erotic Stimulation

The basic configuration for the range of woman-on-top positions is for the man to be lying on his back and the woman to straddle him. She can be facing forward, sideways, or backward. The majority of these positions call for the woman to be facing forward for eye contact, kissing, and speaking. Both partners' hands are free to caress, fondle, and rub different parts of the other partner's body. Experiment with moving your legs to one side or the other while riding your partner. One knee up, one knee down, then switching, is a great combination.

FACT

The face-to-face positions are also the best for G-spot stimulation. As a woman, you can control the depth of thrusting to place the lingam in just the right spot for your best stimulation. Whether you like deep, shallow, or a combination of thrusts, you can facilitate your own experience by being on top.

Face-to-Face Positions

Face-to-face positions are the most intimate of the woman-on-top positions. Both lovers can see each other to kiss and speak. They can witness each other's powerful erotic nature and see the beauty each other has. The flush of the skin, the tiny jewel drops of perspiration, the softly glowing eyes of the lover are all precious visuals that keep the couple engaged and aroused in love play.

Variations on the Prime Position

Both the Kama Sutra and the Ananga Ranga bring you a variety of positions to fuel your passion and imagination. When astride your partner, try leaning down on top of his chest with your knees on the bed. This particular position is a good one for clitoral stimulation because the two of you can rub against each other. With your hands under his shoulders, you can guide your lover in the speed of rubbing to apply maximum friction where you need it most. This is one of the only positions where you can get direct stimulation of the clitoris without the use of the hands.

With your knees on the bed, sit up on your lover. There is a great range of motion with this position because you can move up and down on your partner, as well as forward and backward. Use your hands to apply pressure to your lover's chest for movement, and also caress your lover's face and body.

"When the woman swings her hips and abdomen on all sides, including back and forth and side to side or in circular movements, it is called The Swing" (Part 2, Chapter 8, Sutra 27). This movement is like a belly dancer's hips swaying. If you don't feel confident about this, then practice a few belly-dance moves on your own and then bring your hips back to the bedroom to try the moves out. These movements can be used in a great variety of situations to add stimulus and imagination to your lovemaking.

It's important to focus on clitoral stimulation for most women before intercourse. In a survey taken in 2000 on tantra.com, less than 42 percent of 1,048 women said that they usually or always had vaginal orgasms during intercourse.

Try putting your feet on the bed as you sit astride your lover. This allows you to raise and lower yourself onto your partner. The Kama Sutra calls this position the "Fluttering and Soaring Butterfly" because the woman is in control of the rhythm, depth of thrusting, speed, and angle of penetration. It takes strong thighs to maintain it for any length of time. The man can use his hands to help support the woman and guide her timing.

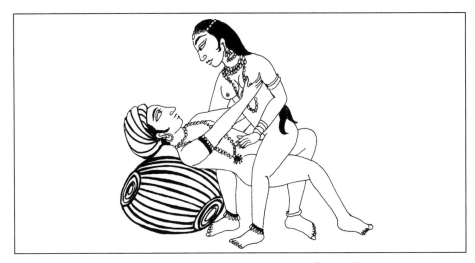

▲ The Fluttering and Soaring Butterfly Position

▲ A variation on the Fluttering and Soaring Butterfly

Next, try one leg with the foot on the bed and the other with the knee on the bed. This position is useful when a woman likes one side of her vagina or G-spot stimulated more than another. It's also very powerful for you to put your hand under your lover's buttocks on the side with the foot on the bed. Pull him gently closer and rock him back and forth. Try both sides.

Unique Positions from the Old Texts

Both of the well-known Indian erotic texts contain unique postures with evocative names. Notice in some of them the use of animal names and plant references. Drawing comparisons to nature is a wonderful practice that the Asian love arts did well. Here are a few:

- "If, drawing up her feet, she revolves her hips so that your penis circles deep within her yoni, you arching your body to help her, it is The Bee."
- "Catching your penis, the lady with dark eyes like upturned lotus petals guides it into her yoni, clings to you and shakes her buttocks: this is Lovely Lady in Control."
- "Enthroned on your penis, she places both hands on the bed and makes love, while you press your two hands to her thudding heart: this is Seat of Sport."
- "Clasping each other's hands, you lie sprawled like two starfish making love, her breasts stabbing your chest, her thighs stretched out along yours: this is The Coitus of the Gods."

Face-to-Feet Positions

Though not as common, some women and men like these positions because of the view they offer to the man. They aren't as effective in reaching the G-spot, but they are great for deeper thrusting for women who like to have the cervix area stimulated during intercourse. They can be intimate when the variations used are the ones where both are sitting, and the man holds the woman close as she sits on his lap. They are especially good if you hang a mirror on the wall so that the two of you can see yourselves. Here are a few:

- "If you lie flat on your back with legs stretched out and your lover sits astride you, facing away and grasping your feet, it is called The Bull."

- "If she strides you, facing your feet, brings both her feet up to your thighs, and works her hips frantically, it is known as Swan Sport."
- "Your lover places one foot on your ankle, lodges her other foot just above your knee, and rides you, swinging and rotating her hips, it is known as Garuda—the Bird."

In many of these positions the woman can place her feet or her knees on the bed. Try the one-foot and one-knee stance as in the front-facing positions. Lean forward or backward for more variety and G-spot stimulation.

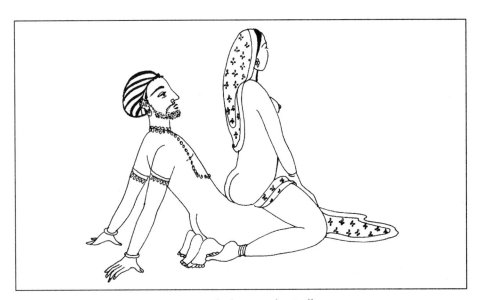

▲ A variation on the Bull

Challenging Positions

The more challenging positions can be a lot of fun to try when the two of you are in a light mood and ready for some adventure. It will help to be very limber and to have a few big pillows around for extra support when needed. Be careful when trying some of these—don't fall off the bed.

Many of these positions are from another well-known Hindu love manual called the Ananga Ranga, which was also translated by Sir

Richard Burton of England. Throughout the ages, the love postures from both the Ananga Ranga and the Kama Sutra have been intertwined. Their addition here gives a much deeper background of information. Some are very interesting indeed.

Women, when you are on top, remember to be careful with your partner's lingam. In your enthusiasm you'll need to make sure that you don't damage it by bouncing down too hard. If it gets caught a little off center and you bend it, it can cause damage to the sensitive blood-holding regions. Play it safe by keeping it in the yoni.

The Swan

"She sits upright upon you, her head thrown back like a rearing mare, bringing her feet together on the bed to one side of your body: this is called The Swan." Depending on which side you might put your two legs, this position could greatly affect your G-spot. You'll need to use your hands to support yourself and to be able to move up and down on your partner.

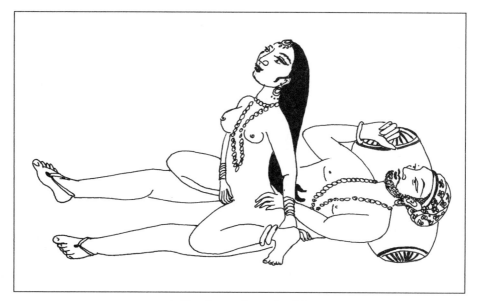

▲ The Swan Sport Position

The Sacred Thread and Reversed

"The young woman has one foot on your heart and the other on the bed. Bold, saucy women adore this posture, which is known to the world as The Sacred Thread." This is a wonderful name. It is derived from the fact that the woman is making a sacred connection with her foot to the man's heart. This connects them and binds the love and other-worldliness of the sexual union.

"If, with one of her feet clasped in your hand and the second placed upon your shoulder, your young lady enjoys you, it is called Reversed." This is a hard position to understand. If you try it, be careful!

The man can help in any of the woman-superior positions by cupping his hands under your buttocks and lifting you up and down. It's fun to have the help and the two of you can dance in the interplay of figuring out the rhythm and speed. It is especially appreciated when your thighs get tired.

The Foot Yoke

"If your lover, seated above you with feet lotus-crossed and her body held erect and still makes love to you, it is known as The Foot Yoke." You will definitely need your partner to help you move up and down with this position. Just getting into the Lotus Position on top of your lover while he keeps his erection is challenging. Your love muscles will need to be in great shape for this one.

The Wheel

"Lying upon you, your beloved moves round like a wheel, pressing hands one after the other on the bed, kissing your body as she circles: experts call this The Wheel." This posture or position is similar to "The Foot Yoke" except that the woman lies down on the man when she moves all the way around him. Positions like these can hurt the woman if she isn't careful about the angle that the penis is penetrating the vagina. Sometimes the male/female combination that you and your partner make isn't conducive to this kind of movement. It can hurt the woman by having the insides of her yoni bumped by the lingam at certain angles.

Women's Worries

Many women say that they avoid being on top because they don't feel confident about how their bodies look. They believe that their breasts sag or their tummy is the first thing their man sees. They worry about the children coming in, or the phone ringing, or that they might crush their partners. The worrying gives them the excuse to not take the initiative. Control can be a little frightening.

ALERT!

The Kama Sutra repeats often that once lovemaking commences, all rules and sutras fly out the door. Let that happen to you when you make love. Abandon inhibitions that keep you from trying erotic new ideas.

Body Issues

Men love breasts hanging in their visual field. If you are really worried, try some positions early on that don't let your breasts hang as much. The positions where the woman puts both of her feet on the bed or floor, on either side of the man, are good because your body is more upright and your knees keep your breasts from hanging. This position takes very strong legs, though, to maintain it for any length of time.

Eventually, you'll need to just trust that your lover wants to see your body and thinks it is beautiful. Men generally love having their lovers take control. You are creating a fantasy come true.

If he seems critical of you, use the communication tools in Chapter 20 to create an opening in which to be heard. State your fears and be vulnerable. Love is created when you drop your defensive pattern and become soft and open.

The Everyday Worries

Women worry about different things than men. While men tend to worry about things such as work, being a good provider, and being a virile lover, women often worry about the children, if the oven got turned off, what someone might think of her, do her thighs jiggle, and whether she is being a good lover.

There really aren't many "right" things when it comes to sex, though. Fun, depth, adventure, and losing oneself in union with the other are all the right things, not techniques. When you practice focusing on pleasurable sensations in yourself, you'll get out of your head and into the bed.

Tricks and Treats

The woman-superior positions allow you to maneuver your hips, thighs, upper body, and yoni muscles to bring great pleasure to both yourself and your lover. This movement can occur as wild, energetic thrusting, or as quiet, subtle actions that stem from the squeezing of the love muscles—or a combination of both. The sexually experienced woman can bring heightened pleasure to a union by practicing these skills and allowing herself the freedom to assume control at times during lovemaking.

Using will and intent in your life can help you have a better sex life! Also, cultivating intention can lead to a more satisfying sex life. Start by focusing on the little things in life and developing skills that keep you moving toward what you want out of life.

"When she takes the man's role, your lady has the choice of three famous lovemaking techniques: The Tongs, The Spinning of the Top, and The Swing" (Part 2, Chapter 8, Sutra 23). These techniques can be used with other positions while the woman is on top. Strong PC (pubococcygeus) muscles will provide any woman with the skills to add variety and excitement to any positions or situation.

◀ A good position for
the Mare's Trick

"If she uses the Mare's Trick, gripping your penis with her yoni's vice, squeezing and stroking it, holding it inside her for a hundred heartbeats, it is known as The Tongs" (Part 2, Chapter 8, Sutra 24). "When, while engaged in congress, she turns round and round like a wheel, it is called The Spinning of the Top" (Part 2, Chapter 8, Sutra 25). This move requires a lot of practice and the woman needs to be small in size. She supports herself and moves around the man with pressure on his chest and legs. "When the woman swings her hips and abdomen on all sides, including back and forth and side to side or in circular movements, it is called The Swing" (Part 2, Chapter 8, Sutra 27).

All of these variations can be easily moved through, like a dance, as the lovemaking progresses. You can perfect this dance by staying aware, limber, and by sometimes leading and sometimes letting your partner lead. Remember to use your hands liberally to caress and fondle your partner. ⒠

Chapter 10

Man-Superior Positions

When your mind drifts toward fantasizing about sex and intercourse, it probably automatically pictures the woman under the man. This basic position is relied on more than any other in the human repertoire of lovemaking. Ancient cultures of the East have expanded upon it and refined the basic man-on-top position to become so much more than its original self.

The Missionary Position

The basic man-on-top position was undoubtedly the first position, other than the rear-entry position, that our very ancient ancestors used. In the Victorian era, a husband rarely saw his wife's body. Her nightclothes so fully covered her body that the only way they could have sex was for the man to insert his penis in the small opening sewn into the very front of her garment. Under such restrictive conditions, the only thing possible was the Missionary Position.

In this basic position, the woman lies on her back with her legs bent, feet on the bed, and knees pointing up. Her partner lies on top of her, generally with his knees on the bed or other surface as he supports himself with his arms. The man does the thrusting and most of the movement in this position. It's a somewhat difficult position for the woman to move freely in, especially if the man is larger than she is and leans on her during lovemaking.

Other basic variations include having the woman wrap her legs over the ankles, thighs, or buttocks of her partner. She can even move them up to his waist and back. These variations sometimes happen spontaneously as the woman gets more excited and turned on. The natural reaction is to move closer to create more contact as the lovemaking progresses.

The Missionary Position can stimulate the G-spot, as well as the interior vaginal spots that women identify as pleasure producing. It's great for eye contact, whispers, loving words, and kissing. However, it generally doesn't do much for women who need clitoral stimulation to orgasm.

Coital Alignment Technique (C.A.T.)

The Coital Alignment Technique (C.A.T.) was developed to provide more stimulation to the clitoral area of the woman's vulva. It involves the same basic position as the Missionary except that the man rises up and moves about four inches closer to the woman's head (up her body) with his body. From this position he can use a combination of small thrusts and rubbing his body up and down her body. Putting pillows under the woman's midriff, to give an arch to her back, helps expose the clitoris to more stimulation.

The rubbing action, which both partners can do in rhythm with each other, presses the man's pubic bone on the woman's pubic bone and clitoral hood. This friction adds enough contact with the clitoris to have her reach orgasm in the act of intercourse. Generally, the C.A.T. Position has partners very close, with arms around each other, so that they can create the traction to get the up-and-down rhythm going. It's this back-and-forth friction that excites the woman. This position may make the man last longer, too, because he isn't creating a lot of direct friction on the shaft of his penis.

FACT

More women experience clitoral orgasms than vaginal or G-spot orgasms. Between 26 to 46 percent of all women say that they have never had an orgasm of any kind. Most women eventually begin to have orgasms at some point in their lives, but not necessarily every time they have intercourse.

Ten Types of Strokes

The Kama Sutra distinguishes ten types of movements that the lingam can do while in the yoni. It calls these movements "strokes," though some of them seem more forceful than the name implies. Each of these, in turn, has multiple variations for enthralling lovers.

"During lovemaking, ten types of strokes may be struck with the penis, but of these only Upasripta (Natural), which is instinctive even to untutored cowherds, results in full clitoral stimulation" (Part 2, Chapter 7, Sutra 11). The Kama Sutra refers to the most common movement of the penis in the vagina: in-and-out at varying speeds, angles, and depths. However, this type of thrusting doesn't necessarily effect the stimulation of the clitoris.

The clitoris is in an awkward spot on the vulva of the woman. It does get some stimulation from the in-and-out action of the penis, but unless the two partners rub in an up-and-down fashion, it isn't likely to get a lot of quality attention. Some angles and positions are better than others for clitoral arousal.

Moving the Organ Forward

"When it is done mildly and naturally, it is called: Moving the Organ Forward" (Part 2, Chapter 7, Sutra 12). This is a gentle forward stroke, which may be varied with depth and speed, allowing subtlety, rhythm, and spontaneity. The other nine lack the range of diversity that this strike has. There is infinite variety in this simple, natural expression of love.

Churning and Piercing

"If you grasp your penis and move it in circles inside her yoni, it is: Churning" (Part 2, Chapter 7, Sutra 13). To try this one, find positions that allow the man to support himself easily so that he has a free hand to "churn" with. This kind of stroke may be highly enjoyable to some women because it will be relatively shallow penetration. The G-spot may likely be stimulated.

◀ A good G-spot position

Piercing happens when "the yoni is lowered and the man unites from a higher angle" (Part 2, Chapter 7, Sutra 14). This is a good clitoris stroke. With the woman's hips lower, so that even her middle area is raised, she is exposing her clitoris more fully.

When the man is above his partner, the angle of penetration will rub his pubic bone on her pubic bone, near her clitoris. This is the basic idea behind the C.A.T. mentioned earlier.

Rubbing and Pressing

"If, when her hips are raised by a pillow, and the man is lower, you strike a rising blow, it is Rubbing" (Part 2, Chapter 7, Sutra 15). This is a good G-spot stroke. The head of the lingam is angled upward, and the woman's hips are raised so that the tip presses in the area of the G-spot.

"If you hold your penis pressed breathlessly to her womb it is called: Pressing" (Part 2, Chapter 7, Sutra 16). Pressing and holding for a few seconds provides a wonderful chance to "milk" the penis with your PC (pubococcygeus) muscles for a more subtle stimulation. This may also provide some friction for the clitoris, especially if you slightly rub your bodies together.

Giving a Blow

"If you withdraw slightly and then strike her deeply to the womb, it is called: Giving a Blow" (Part 2, Chapter 7, Sutra 17). Many women like deep thrusting because of an area near the cervix, in the back of the vagina. They say that they are very sensitive there, and this area may even trigger orgasm. Women of the Deer type (or with shallow vaginas) will not like this move unless they are partnered with a man who matches their size in genitals. If it hurts, don't do this one.

The Boar's and Bull's Blows

"Continuous pressure on one side of her yoni is: The Boar's Blow" (Part 2, Chapter 7, Sutra 18). This kind of an angle can provide a tighter fit for the man, but it may not be particularly comfortable for the woman. It may work better with the penis deep inside the vagina.

"If you thrust wildly in every direction, like a bull tossing its horns, it is: The Bull's Blow" (Part 2, Chapter 7, Sutra 19). When passion takes over, this pattern of stroking might come into play. Do not allow the lingam to come out of the vagina too often. The risk is bending or hurting the shaft of the penis if it glances sideways and misses the yoni. This might be painful for the woman, too.

FACT

The vagina has only a couple of very sensitive spots inside. The sides of the yoni aren't considered highly sensitive or even erotic to some women.

The Sporting of the Sparrow and Clasping

"When the lingam is in the yoni, and is moved up and down frequently, and without being taken out, it is called: The Sporting of the Sparrow" (Part 2, Chapter 7, Sutra 20). Vatsyayana indicates that this move is done near the end of lovemaking. It signifies a "quickening" on the part of the man. He is generally in the eighth or ninth zone, on a scale of 1 to 10. Women, if you notice your partner in this kind of a move, and you are working on ejaculation mastery together, slow him down now. Have him look into your eyes, kiss, and even breathe together, to relax you for a few minutes. Then, begin again.

"When the union is affected without withdrawing the penis and both the woman and the man lie united and press their thighs to each other it is called: Clasping" (Part 2, Chapter 7, Sutra 21). Both lovers lie still in this position. It is necessary to use the skills of the woman to pump her PC muscles in order to continue the stimulation.

The Man-on-Top Postures

In the man-on-top postures, the hands are generally free to stimulate other erogenous zones. The man can use his hands and fingers on the clitoris, the breasts, the face, the heart, or any other area on the woman's body where he knows her pleasure will be enhanced. The woman is free to ask for the touch that she would like. The woman's hands are also available to caress her partner's face, back, neck, thighs and legs, and scrotum, or to gently pull his hair or wrap her arms around his neck.

She can assist him in having an orgasm but not ejaculating in these positions because she can read his energy easily. She is able to move, do her Kegels to grip him firmly, or lie still so he won't ejaculate too soon. If appropriate, she can pump her PC muscles slowly and keep her partner just at the edge of excitement. This is a good way to let the man come back to a more stable state if he is feeling that he might be getting close to ejaculating.

In recent years, lovemaking pillows of various sizes and shapes have come on the market. There are even a few manufacturers of "love furniture." These are ideal to use during lovemaking, since their shapes can be molded to fit your needs.

The Widely Open Position

This position is recommended for the "Deer"-type woman who tends to have a smaller-size vagina. You can read more about the categories of men and women in Chapter 14. "When she lowers her head and raises her middle parts, it is called: Widely Open Position. At such a time the man should apply some unguent (lubrication), so as to make the entrance easy" (Part 2, Chapter 6, Sutra 8). You might almost want to invert the woman slightly in this position. Her head should be lower than her hips by a little, and her legs should be relaxed and open wide. This posture opens up her yoni to receive the lingam better.

The Yawning Position

"When the woman raises her legs and her thighs and keeps them wide apart and engages in congress, it is called: the Yawning Position" (Part 2, Chapter 6, Sutra 10). With the man on top, you can go from the Missionary Position to the Yawning Position very easily; or you can begin in the Yawning Position. Thrusting should begin gently, as this is a vulnerable position for some women.

▲ The Yawning Position

Here is a great variation. The woman lies on her back and places her legs up and over the shoulders of her partner, who is on top of her. The legs can rest on his shoulders with very little strain to the man. This is only a moderately difficult position for the woman. She should not use a pillow, if any, under her buttocks, as this will limit her mobility.

With her legs on his shoulders, she will have the leverage to lift her pelvis easily and affect the angle of penetration. The woman can rotate her hips easily for maximum contact to her G-spot. The rotating also stimulates the man, and so they can both easily control the movement and the thrusting.

Another variation on this position has the woman take her legs off the man's shoulders and straighten her legs. She then firmly pushes the backs of her legs away from the man, so that her feet move closer to her head. She can use her hands to push against his chest. In doing so, she puts an even greater angle on her pelvis, and consequently the man's penis accesses the G-spot better. The woman is more in control of the thrusting in this variation. She can control the deep versus shallow thrusts and the speed of the thrusting when she pushes with her hands on his chest. This is a little more difficult for some women, but try it before you decide that it's not for you. The more of an angle you are able to put on the vagina and penis, the more pressure will be applied to the G-spot and penis, causing greater pleasure.

The Yawning Position is excellent for accessing the G-spot, and the woman will have the benefit of very direct G-spot stimulation. Because the two of you are very close in proximity, the breath can be watched closely and communication is easy.

Splitting a Bamboo Position

"When the woman places one of her legs on her lover's shoulder, and stretches the other out, and then places the latter on his shoulder, and stretches the other out, and continues to do so alternately, it is called: The Splitting of a Bamboo" (Part 2, Chapter 6, Sutra 26). The woman lies on her back and can be propped up by pillows placed at her back. Her partner squats, kneels, or sits on his feet with a slightly forward tilt.

▲ Beginning position for Splitting of a Bamboo

The woman has one leg bent with her foot on the floor or bed. The other leg is on the man's shoulder, with the ankle hooked on the shoulder of the man or straight up in the air and held by her partner's hand. At the couple's own pace, one leg is then shifted and the opposite mirror image of the position is assumed. As in the Kama Sutra description, the legs are at one moment split one way and then the other way. This one's more on the advanced level, but give it a try. You may surprise yourself.

The Splitting of a Bamboo is a wonderful position for making the subtle shifts often required for effective G-spot stimulation. The woman can grind and rotate her hips, or use her PC muscles to create greater pleasure. The up-and-down movement of the legs causes an arc to be created that rubs, like the motion of a windshield wiper, back and forth across the G-spot area.

Posture of Indrani

"Indrani draws up both her knees until they nuzzle the curves of her breasts; her feet find her lover's armpits. Small girls love this posture, but becoming a goddess takes a lot of practice" (Part 2, Chapter 6, Sutra 11). This is an advanced position and requires a very limber body. The woman's legs are pressed to her sides and the man can alternate kneeling with supporting himself on one foot or the other.

This is also a good G-spot posture. The angle of penetration favors the upper portion of the woman's vagina where the G-spot is located. This is a great position for lovers when the man has an unusually large penis.

▲ The Posture of Indrani Position

The Rising Position

"Grasping the ankles of the round-hipped woman, whose buttocks are like two ripe gourds, raise her beautiful thighs and spread the thigh-joints widely it is called: The Rising Position" (Part 2, Chapter 6, Sutra 22). In this position, it helps if the man is strong. He will be moving the woman up and down on him, partially with the use of his arms.

The Pressed and Half-Pressed Positions

"When the man bends the woman's legs and presses them down with his bosom, it is: the Pressed Position" (Part 2, Chapter 6, Sutra 24). In this posture, the woman scrunches up her legs and places her feet on the man's chest. She pushes against him and he holds her feet in place by exerting pressure back. This is a more advanced position because of the limberness required on the part of the woman.

"When only one of her legs is stretched out in the above position, it is called: The Half-Pressed Position" (Part 2, Chapter 6, Sutra 25). This is a good posture for experimenting with G-spot stimulation. If you try this position, investigate which side you like to stretch your leg out to. You may like one side or the other. This would indicate that one side of your upper yoni has a little more sensitivity for your G-spot than the other.

Which positions do you prefer?
Try three new positions from each of the positions chapters and then rate them. Have your partner rate his or hers separately and then compare. See which ones you both have on your lists.

The Fixing a Nail Position

"When one of her legs is placed on the head, or near it, and the other is stretched out, it is called: the Fixing of a Nail. It is learned only by practice" (Part 2, Chapter 6, Sutra 27). This is a difficult posture and one that should not be forced but worked into naturally. It takes a supple body and mind. If you try, find a variation on it that you can manage and then work toward the more difficult original position.

▲ The Fixing a Nail Position

The Ananga Ranga

Though written much later, the Ananga Ranga is a companion book to the Kama Sutra. Its recommendations, wisdom, and positions add to the knowledge that came from the Kama Sutra. The sweet, transformative names given to some of the positions described by the Ananga Ranga speak to the possibility of full, erotic expression.

The Ananga Ranga beseeches the man to learn to time himself so that his partner is fully satisfied. By assuming postures or positions that allow him to both pleasure her and control himself, he pleasures her more completely. Women need more arousal time to come to orgasm. The man who can master her orgasmic timing and his own timing is a gift to his partner.

"One of man's chief duties is to learn to withhold himself as much as possible and the same time to hasten the enjoyment of his partner. The desires of the woman are cooler and slower to rouse than those of the man; she is not easily satisfied by a single act of lovemaking. Her slower excitement demands prolonged embraces, and if these are denied her, then she often feels irritated. By the second love-act the passions of the woman become fully aroused and she has a full orgasm; then she can be said to be contented. This state of affairs is reversed in the case of a man, who approaches the first act burning with love-heat, which cools during the second, often leaving him languid and disinclined for a third." —The Ananga Ranga

Positions of the Ananga Ranga

Here is a taste of some of the positions that the Ananga Ranga has to offer. The names are interesting and often suggestive of transformation and pleasure.

In the Elixir Position, the woman opens her legs up, places her knees and feet fairly high in the air, and the man squats in front of her. He puts both hands on her lower back and buttocks and draws her very near. They can gently rock in this position.

In the Remembrance Wheel Position, the woman lies on her back and the man squats close in between her legs. She puts her legs out on the bed and the man holds them out as far as they will go. He maneuvers her body by manipulating her legs with his hands. Her hands are free to caress him and stimulate her clitoris.

▲ The Remembrance Wheel Position

The Inexhaustible Kindness Position requires the woman to lie with pillows to prop her up and with legs up and knees out. She places her feet near the man's chest and he squats near her. A variation has the man place one of his feet farther forward than the other so that he can get in closer to his lover.

Here is a list of some other Ananga Ranga positions:

- "She bends well forward and grips the bedstead, her buttocks raised high; cup your hands to serpents' hoods and squeeze her jar-shaped breasts together, this is: The Milk Cow."
- "If she lies on her stomach and you seize her ankles in one hand, lift them high and make love, tilting her chin back with your other hand, it is: The Cat."
- "She lies on her front, grasping her ankles in her own hands and pulling them up behind her: this difficult posture is known to experts as: The Wrestler."
- "Seize her feet and lift them high (like a wheel barrow), drive your penis into her yoni and pleasure her with vigorous strokes: this is The Thunderbolt."
- "You kneel, as in archery, take her on your lap and bend her forward till her breasts are pressed to her thighs: this is One Knot."

Men Who Gain Success with Women

The Kama Sutra includes a list that contains the kinds of men who tend to attract women. The list is preceded by numerous ways in which a man can win the heart of a woman he is wooing.

Men who can gain success with women tend to be experts at the arts of love. They have experience and knowledge of a woman's body and her sexual needs. Women are attracted to men who are mature, obedient, and soft spoken. If a woman knows a man from childhood, trusts him with her secrets, and he is liberal with his gifts, she will be drawn to him.

According to the Kama Sutra, women prefer men who are good at playing games, narrating tales and episodes from the great myths and holy books, and who are fond of dramatic performances. Some women are drawn to men who are sought after by another woman, superior to her in society. A man is said to be desirable if he is of the Bull type, in other words, if he has a large penis. You can visit Chapter 14 for more information on the genital types of men and women that the Kama Sutra describes.

Women also like men who are adventurous, brave, and good-looking. One who has knowledge, good fortune, is comfortable, and who dresses and behaves in an aristocratic manner is very lucky in love. Having a capacity for enjoyment of society, friends, family, and his lover makes a man attractive and desirable.

"Desire, which springs from nature, and which is increased by art, and from which all danger is taken away by wisdom, becomes firm and secure" (Part 5, Chapter 1, Sutra 53). Love born through mutual regard and nurtured attention survives many crises. And, "A clever man, depending on his own ability, and observing carefully the ideas and thoughts of women, and removing the causes of their turning away from men, is generally successful with them" (Part 5, Chapter 1, Sutra 54).

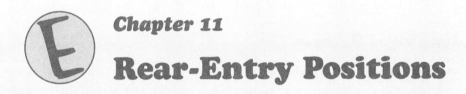

Chapter 11

Rear-Entry Positions

Without a doubt, the rear-entry is one of the best sets of sexual positions. The Kama Sutra thought highly of nature and so the text suggested that erotic explorers study animals' ways of lovemaking. The rear-entry positions are the result of those studies, with added sophistication from thousands of years of further research.

Animal-like Behavior in Bed

There is a certain stigmatism about the more "animal-like" behaviors during sex, for some people. For whatever reasons—societal, parental, or maybe an experience that didn't go well—you may be reluctant to attempt some of these. Try suspending your judgments sometime soon and invite your lover to an evening of adventure.

Advantages Galore

Rear-entry positions enhance G-spot stimulation. They have the advantage of leaving the hands free to caress and fondle the breasts, buttocks, and back. Variety is easy to come by in these positions, too.

You can adjust the angle and depth of penetration and the ways you move. This allows the woman to tailor the experience for herself while having a lot of room to increase the pleasure for her partner. It also enables the woman or the man to stimulate her clitoris. For some women, this is an important part of intercourse.

Men may find increased control in these positions, which will assist them in lasting longer. You can be in control of the depth, speed, and rhythm. You have a wonderful, archetypal view of your partner, reminiscent of ancient or primitive man. Men can feel powerful and still maintain sensitivity with their partner.

Choosing the Right Time

Rear-entry positions aren't always the most appropriate, however. The moment must be right. Sometimes it's just more appropriate to be facing each other. Eye contact, breath connection, heart connection, and intimacy are all facilitated through facing your partner.

If either of you has issues or is sensitive about trying some of these positions, you'll need to talk. Be open with each other and vulnerable when you speak. If you are, your partner will hear you better and be more compassionate. Even with reservations, try a few of these. If you have to push yourself over the edge a little, know that it's a good learning experience. You may love it.

Types of Rear-Entry Positions

The Kama Sutra names the rear-entry positions after animals, as this is their natural source. This adds a creative, evocative essence to them. It even goes as far as to suggest that couples mimic the sounds and attitudes of the animals that inspired the position.

The Deer

"If the lady, eager for love, goes on all fours, humping her back like a doe, and you enjoy her from behind, rutting as though you'd lost all human nature, it is called: The Deer." Try this position first with both partners on their knees. It's best for the woman to support herself with both her hands, on all fours, so that she can keep her spine moving and undulating. Use the different rhythms and depths of penetration to explore how this basic position feels to both of you.

A great variation on this position is for the woman to lift one of her legs so that her lover can hold it up for her. Alternate lifting each leg as one will most likely be more effective than the other. Make a study of how it feels, and communicate your findings to your lover for future reference.

The Dog

"If you mount her like a dog, gripping her waist, and she twists round to gaze into your face, experts in the art of love say it is: The Dog." The variations on all of these positions lend themselves well to different locations around the house and yard. Try this position on a padded chair or the couch.

The Elephant

"When your mistress lays breasts, arms, and forehead to the carpet, raising her buttocks high, and you guide your penis into her yoni, it is called: The Elephant." Though this isn't a great G-spot position, it has many advantages. It is restful and comfortable, and also very erotic. If you like your partner to play with and stimulate your anal area, this is a great position.

This is also a good position for stimulating the man by caressing his scrotum or his inner thighs. You can help him stay focused on nonejaculatory pleasure by cupping his scrotum in your hands and gently applying pressure with a downward pull. You can apply pressure to his perineum area also, which is the exterior access to his prostate gland.

The "love handles," or waistline area of the torso, are exquisite erogenous zones. Hold on here often and even caress the sides of the torso from under the arms all the way down the sides to the hips. Holding on firmly in this area, to facilitate thrusting, is very erotic for both the man and the woman.

▲ The Elephant Position

The Reverse Monkey Position

"The round-thighed woman on the bed grasps her ankles and raises high her lotus feet; you strike her to the root, kissing and slapping open-palmed between her breasts—this is The Monkey." A much easier variation on this position has the man sit back on his thighs and the woman sit back on top of him, still in the rear-entry position. Men should try putting one hand on their partner's heart and one on the lower part of her stomach in this position. Hold her close and undulate like a wave, connected at the core. This is a great G-spot posture.

◀ The Monkey Position

Some Different Modalities to Try

Try pumping and squeezing your PC muscles in some of these positions. Both of you can do this to see how it feels. Try breathing in sync and squeezing together. Add some of the thrusting pattern variations from Chapter 8. Keep a small hand mirror available somewhere near your bed so that the two of you can eye gaze as you get more and more aroused.

Ask yourselves how you are doing often when trying new positions. Don't assume that your partner is having a good time without asking. When you try new things ask: "What has changed?" Both of you take notice of any subtle changes. Is your G-spot as stimulated in this position? Do you find it easier to rise up and down on your partner? What do you notice in each of these?

Penetration can be quite deep in rear-entry positions. Make sure your "fit" isn't hurting her. If she moves away from you, in little increments, you'll know something is wrong. Women who are having their periods may find more discomfort during those times than normally.

Standing Rear-Entry Positions

The Kama Sutra makes note of just one rear-entry position. "When a woman stands on her hands and feet like a quadruped, and her lover mounts her like a bull, it is called: the Congress of the Cow. At this time everything that is ordinarily done on the bosom should be done on the back" (Part 2, Chapter 6, Sutras 37–38). It then goes on to say, "In the same way can be carried on the congress of the dog, the congress of the goat, the congress of a deer, the forcible mounting of an ass, the congress of a cat, the jump of a tiger, the pressing of an elephant, the rubbing of a boar, and the mounting of a horse. And in all of these the characteristics of the different animals should be manifested by acting like them" (Part 2, Chapter 6, Sutra 39).

Rear-entry positions are excellent G-spot–stimulating positions. Because both partners can maneuver their bodies so well, access to the G-spot can become very precise.

The Lending-an-Arm Position

The couch or overstuffed chair will always be more than happy to lend you an arm. Lean over the arm as you stand on the floor. Your lover will stand behind you. You can also try kneeling on both knees on the chair near the edge.

The Stork

Try a standing position next to the arm of a comfortable chair by holding on to the chair arm, bending over slightly, and lifting either your right or left leg into the air while your lover enters you. Lift your leg straight back behind you so that your lover can hold it by his side and use it as a lever arm to move you to and fro. Experiment with different legs held high and then low. You'll probably find that one of your legs is better than the other. You'll notice more friction in just the area you need it on your G-spot.

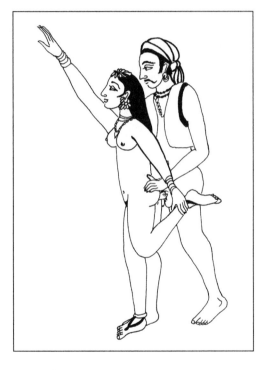

◀ The Stork Rear-Entry
Position

The Ass

"When, with lotus-feet set well-apart on the ground, she bends, placing a hand upon each thigh, and you take her from the rear, it is called: "The Ass." The man should caress and hold the woman's waist so that she doesn't fall forward in this position. This position takes a strong limber body.

Tricks and Tips

For the very erotic couple these positions will be exciting. You'll be able to find subtle variations that will suit you as a couple and add new, creative extras to get even more out of this group of love postures. Here are a few tips to help you fantasize and get your creative juices started.

The Mirror

In the past, couples have used mirrors for a variety of reasons during lovemaking. They can be seen in old Chinese Taoist drawings being used by couples that wished to study their faces while in orgasmic pleasure. The Taoists felt that is was important to be able to witness oneself in the act of pleasure in order to understand better the nature of one's own bliss.

You can use a hand mirror or mount one or two mirrors on your bedroom walls. The hand mirror is intimate because you can pick it up and have it very close to your faces. In rear-entry positions, you can both look into it and see each other. It makes a very exciting and intimate picture of the two of you. Have the woman hold it in front of the couple.

▲ Using a mirror to eye gaze

The Bed Bar

Using a bar suspended above the bed or using a high headboard can be very erotic and fun when trying rear-entry positions. If the woman can get a higher angle on the lingam inside of her by holding herself up on the headboard or bar, she can put more stimulation on her G-spot. She can also assist her man in thrusting because she can pull herself up and down with her hands.

Involving the Scrotum in Lovemaking

Many men love to have their scrotum gently pulled during lovemaking because it can help them control their ejaculation and will add increased pleasure to the experience. But it is often difficult to get into a position that allows this kind of activity. Some of the rear-entry postures make it easier to reach his genitals for this stimulating addition.

FACT

Throughout history lovers have used sex toys and enhancers that have been developed for various reasons. The use of a soft, restrictive device around the base of the penis can increase the amount of blood that stays in the penis during sex, thus creating a firmer erection. A common term for this is a "cock ring."

Be gentle and always ask first if it is something he would like to try. You may also wish to apply pressure to his perineum (the external area between the anus and the scrotum that covers his prostate gland or the male G-spot). This will help keep him from going over the top, so to speak.

Another option is to tie a very slim silk belt or robe tie around his scrotum with a slipknot. String it forward, between his legs, and have the woman hold on to it. She can gently tug and pull on it to increase the pressure and pull on his scrotum.

Positions for Groups

While this isn't the book to go into detail about the practices of groups having sex, the Kama Sutra does include it. Many wealthy men of the time had several wives and some did engage in group sexual experiences. The Kama Sutra also describes situations in which several men met with one courtesan at the same time. Usually, though, one man entertained several women.

The practices were decidedly different then than they are now, although there are some couples and singles who often participate in group sexual experiences. Numerous old paintings and drawings depict one man with two or more women. "When a man enjoys two women at the same time, both of whom love him equally, it is called: The United Congress" (Part 2, Chapter 6, Sutra 40).

FACT

In a survey on tantra.com of 2,400 people, 36 percent of all respondents said they would like to have an experience of having sex with more than one person at a time.

The position known as "The Herd of Cows" is the classic multiwoman experience. "When a man enjoys many women all together, it is called: The Congress of the Herd of Cows" (Part 2, Chapter 6, Sutra 41). Although not a very flattering name, it does get the point across. "Many young men may enjoy a woman that may be married to one of them, either one after the other, or at the same time. Thus one of them holds her, another enjoys her, a third uses her mouth, a fourth holds her middle part, and in this way they go on enjoying her alternately" (Part 2, Chapter 6, Sutra 43).

▲ The Herd of Cows Position

Some promiscuous behavior may have gone on in the harem as well. "The same thing can be done when several men are sitting in the company of one courtesan, or when one courtesan is alone with many men. In the same way this can be done by the women of the king's harem when they accidentally get hold of a man" (Part 2, Chapter 6, Sutras 44–45). The Kama Sutra also suggests that groups can use water or pools for congress, many of which have names that are reminders of animals in herds. Ⓔ

Chapter 12

Sitting, Lying, and Standing Positions

Some of the most sublime, challenging, and relaxing positions can be found in this group of ancient lovemaking postures. From the transformational Tantric Yab/Yum to the mythical standing positions that only a few will try—all are out of the ordinary and extraordinary, too. Using your mind to help your body get into some of these positions will help you feel the soul in them.

Consciousness and Sex

Bringing consciousness to sex isn't something that you are probably used to thinking about. Ancient lovers and philosophers thought otherwise. They believed that through sexuality a person could gain valuable skills and insight into the mind, body, and spirit. Some of the more experimental positions give the opportunity for a couple to stay really tuned in to what they are doing.

It may be easy for you to have pretty good sex by using three or four main positions during intercourse that are familiar to you and your partner. Trying new positions, though, is on the top of the list for most couples that are looking for a new lift to their sex lives. If this is you, you are on the right track.

Positions that are new to you and your partner tend to make you sit up and think a little. You get more conscious. Sometimes you have to use your mind to figure out where a leg goes or what angle is best for stimulation. You have to be more involved than going on habitual behavior. This is always good for a relationship.

If you are afraid of trying new things during sex, but your partner wants to, then try a new position or two. It is the easiest and most enjoyable way to explore new territory in a sexual relationship. Start with easier ones and then move into a few more advanced ones. Stay light, stay alert, and have fun.

Make a list of four new positions from this chapter that appeal to you. If you are the one who is more cautious in the relationship, then pick the order that you will try them. If you are the more adventurous, then let your partner design the order and even pick the positions. Let that person be the leader in this love game.

Sitting Positions

"Sitting erect, grip your lover's waist and pull her on to you, your loins continuously leaping together with a sound like the flapping of elephants' ears: this is called: The Knot of Fame" (The Ananga Ranga). There are only a few actual sitting positions, but they are gems. The ancient Tantric adepts claimed these positions aided in the movement of conscious energy that kept the body healthy and connected them to the gods and goddesses.

Here are examples of a few sitting positions from the Kama Sutra and the Ananga Ranga:

- "Seated, mouth to mouth, arms against arms, thighs against thighs, this is: The Tortoise."
- "If the lovers' thighs, still joined, are raised, it is called: Turning."
- "If, within the cave of her thighs, you sit rotating your hips like a black bee, it is: The Monkey."
- "And if, in this pose, you turn away from her, it is called: Crushing Spices."
- "When your wife sits with both knees drawn tight to her body and you mirror this posture, it is known to experts in the art of love as: The Foot Yoke."
- "Seated erect, the lovely girl folds one leg to her body and stretches the other along the bed, while you mirror her actions: this is: The Feet Yoke."

Yab/Yum Position

The Yab/Yum Position is a little known, but excellent position from the Tantric tradition of India. Lovers sit upon each other face-to-face and heart-to-heart. They are able to keep eye contact, kiss, and caress each other. This position is the best one for extending the sexual experience because it prevents the man from thrusting so much that he ejaculates too quickly. It allows for the deep connection that makes the extended lovemaking experience magical.

In this position, the man sits cross-legged on the bed or floor, and the woman sits astride him. She is facing him and has her legs wrapped around him with the soles of her feet coming together behind him. Both partners have their arms and hands wrapped around the backs of their partner. Their faces are very close. The woman can also put a firm pillow under her buttocks to help with the pressure on her lover's thighs.

◀ The Yab/Yum Position

The lovers are sitting up, in an "awake" position, versus lying down. With the man's penis in the "up" position, the whole energy is vertical. This allows the couple's bodies to move and wave in a freer manner. The breath of each partner can move in synchronicity or they can do alternate breathing for maximum pheromone transmission. The hands of each partner support the other and the man can easily control his urge to ejaculate.

FACT

In the classic Yab/Yum Position, the woman can lean back on pillows and relax as her partner uses his hands to bring her closer for thrusting. His hands are available to caress her clitoris and massage her breasts and thighs.

The Classic Hassock Yab/Yum

You can modify the Yab/Yum posture so that you are really comfortable. If you are unable to do the yogic, cross-legged version of this position, here's another version. You can create the same effect by having the man sit on the edge of the bed or a padded hassock (footstool) with his legs on the floor while the woman sits facing him on his lap. Make sure the man's legs are parallel to the floor from the knees to the hip. This is a good modification for people with lower back problems.

Making Love Like Moths

A Tantric lying-down position that makes reference to moths making love also looks like a Yantra, or Tantric magical symbol. The couple lies down on their backs with the soles of their feet touching, holding their legs in the crooks of their arms. They are close together with buttocks touching and the man's lingam in the woman's yoni.

This is a difficult position and one that requires both partners to be very limber. It may be much easier to start in a sitting position and then recline backward to the lying-down position. Another option is to have just one of you lie back while the other stays sitting. The sitting partner can use his or her hands to caress all the parts of the other partner's body from this position.

Squatting Position

The man must have very strong, limber leg muscles for this one. He squats and she sits astride him, facing him. Her legs are left dangling in air as he supports her. The woman can hold her legs in the crook of her arms, too. He can hold on to a bar or couch arm to help steady them. Subtle movements and rocking achieve the couple's ecstasy.

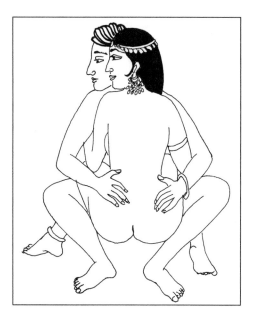

◀ The Squatting Position

Standing Positions

These are the positions that seem mythological and impossible to even think of trying. You may be inclined to skip right over this section, but don't be too sure that there isn't something available to you and your partner, even modified, that might suit you very well in your lovemaking quest.

Some of these positions require that you and your partner be of similar heights because your genitals won't meet if you aren't. However, in others, where the woman is lifted up and isn't using her own feet, your height won't matter.

Supported Congress

"When a couple make love standing, or leaning against a wall or a pillar, it is called Supported Congress" (Part 2, Chapter 6, Sutra 35). Leaning on a wall will make this position much easier to try. You might even want to cheat a little and put a bar stool under the woman, next to the wall. You can then lift her up from that height as you get more turned on and she trusts you've actually got her in your arms.

◀ The Supported Congress
Position

Suspended Congress

"When the woman sits in her lover's cradled hands, her arms around his neck, thighs gripping his waist, her feet pushing back and forth against a wall, it is: Suspended." (Part 2, Chapter 6, Sutra 36). In this posture, the man stands against a wall or anything that will support his back, and the woman sits on his clasped hands as he holds her up. Again, you may want to start from a bar stool or tabletop. She is suspended by his arms and holds herself to him with her own arms around his neck and her legs around his thighs. If she is very small, she can thrust by pushing her feet against the wall that is supporting the man.

In a survey of 2,400 people on tantra.com, 84 percent said that they were interested in learning new positions to try with their partners. It was the most popular thing by far that people wanted to try.

Standing Positions from the Ananga Ranga

The Ananga Ranga, which was a later love manual from India (translated into English by Sir Richard Burton in the 1800s), names additional standing lovemaking postures to the ones the Kama Sutra details. The Kama Sutra is actually a little lean on positions. The Ananga Ranga was used by couples in ancient India as an adjunct to the Kama Sutra.

Here are some examples of standing positions from the Ananga Ranga:

- "When, catching and crushing your lover in the cage of your arms, you force her knees apart with yours and sink slowly into her, it is called: Churning Curds." This is a standing position, but the activity is more of a thrusting technique than an actual position. In certain standing postures, the man has a lot of leeway to move his hips to simulate the Churning Curds.
- "When she leans against a wall, planting her feet as widely apart as possible, and you enter the cave between her thighs, eager for lovemaking, it is: Face-to-Face." You'll both need to be about the same height for this one. You may be able to try it from a sitting position, too, by having the man sit on a hassock with his knees far apart.
- "If, as you lean against the wall, your lady twines her thighs around yours, locks her feet to your knees, and clasps your neck, making love very passionately, it is: The Swing." Lean your shoulders on the wall and have your pelvis tilted out, away from the wall for this one. Keep your knees bent to ease your back.
- "When your lover draws up one leg, allowing the heel to nestle just behind your knee, and you make love, embracing her forcefully, it is: The Stride." It's best to make sure you are bending your knees and

keeping your back straight for this one. This will give you the strength to handle her weight and the pressure on your knee.

- "If you catch one of her knees firmly in your hand and stand making love with her while her hands explore and caress your body, it is called: The Tripod." Both partners stand for this one. The woman places one foot between the man's two feet and lifts the other foot and leg so that her lover can hold her leg at about his waist in height. Hold her leg near the ankle or calf to facilitate thrusting.
- "She stands against the wall, lotus-hands on hips, long, lovely fingers reaching to her navel. Cup her foot in your palm and let your free hand caress your angel's limbs. Put your arm around her neck and enjoy her as she leans there at her ease. Vatsyayana and others, who knew the art of love in its great days, called this posture The Palm. If you lean back on a wall and your lover, clinging to your neck, places both her feet in your palms and thus makes love, this is: Two Palms."
- "If you lift your lover by passing your elbows under her knees and gripping her buttocks while she hangs fearfully from your neck, it called: The Knee Elbow." You may be able to get into this position better if you first use a bar stool or something rather high to lift your lover from.

Hints and Tips

For the right couple, the standing positions may be perfect for practice at gaining ejaculation control for the man. Because they require extra physical consciousness, and it's kind of difficult to relax fully, these postures give a man a little more mindful presence as to his level of excitement. He is in control and he is also responsible for holding both of them up. This may cause just enough distraction to be helpful.

ALERT!

Talk to your partner! It is better to be vulnerable to your fears and state them to your partner than keep them to yourself. Things will not get better if you stay quiet about the issues that cause you to hold back while making love.

◄ A variation on the
Tripod Position

Pleasure swings are similar in this respect. When the woman is suspended in a swing, and the man is standing, the man is freer to move and manage the stimulus to his lingam. He can rest, thrust deeply or more shallowly, slow the pace, and even practice "Churning Curds" using a swing.

Lying-Down Positions

Many of the lying-down positions in the Kama Sutra are recommended for love partnerships where the woman has a large-type yoni and the man a relatively small-size lingam. It is thought that she can make her yoni tighter by closing her legs. Most of these lying-down positions follow that general principle.

It is also true, though, that a woman can accommodate a very large lingam by using these positions to have her thighs act as part of her yoni.

By closing her legs tightly around the lingam, she can "add" to her yoni size by allowing just the tip of the man's penis to actually enter her while the rest is being rubbed by her thighs. This keeps the woman from being hurt and the man thoroughly stimulated.

The lying-down positions may create more friction on the clitoris. More rubbing and squeezing goes on in these positions because there isn't a lot of traction for thrusting. Rubbing, especially on the pubic bone, is what works best for clitoral stimulation in intercourse.

Samputa or Jewel Case Group

The group of positions called the Jewel Case is recommended for lovers who don't have the best of fits. They are termed: the Clasping Position, the Pressing Position, the Twinning Position, and the Mare's Trick. The Mare's Trick isn't really a position—it's a technique.

"In the Clasping Position your legs lie along hers caressing their whole length from toes to thighs. Your lover may be below you, or you may both lie on your sides, in which case she should always be on your left" (Part 2, Chapter 6, Sutra 15). The woman is either below the man or to his side in this position. The variation of the woman on top is discussed in Chapter 9. The legs are kept rather stiff and straight so that the woman's thighs rub the man's penis and her vagina remains contracted.

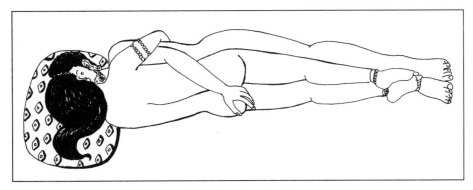

▲ The Clasping Position

"When, after congress has begun in the Clasping Position, the woman presses her lover with her thighs, it is called the Pressing Position" (Part 2, Chapter 6, Sutra 18). The woman can use her hands to pull her lover closer to her and press him by raising her hips a little. He can use his hands to hold and press her breasts. This adds friction and pressure to the thigh area of both. The woman's vagina contracts in size as her abdomen contracts while pressing upward.

"When the woman places one of her thighs across the thigh of her lover, it is called: the Twining Position" (Part 2, Chapter 6, Sutra 19). This is a good position for adjusting the angle of penetration for G-spot stimulation. The man's thigh can rub the clitoris, too. This is a frontal-type position, but if the same idea is utilized while in a Spooning Position from the back it is essentially the same thing—twinning.

▲ The Twinning Position

The Mare's Trick

The Mare's Trick is a technique rather than a position. In fact, it can be employed in almost any position, though it is mentioned in this group because it is especially useful when engaging in these rather quiet positions. "When, like a mare cruelly gripping a stallion, your lover traps and milks your penis with her vagina, it is called: the Mare's Trick, which can only be perfected with long practice" (Part 2, Chapter 6, Sutra 20).

Courtesans were adept at the Mare's Trick. It allowed them to be good lovers with any size man. It is an amazing thing to be able to completely stimulate your partner by just moving, squeezing, and pulsing your PC (pubococcygeus) muscles.

In order to use this technique, you will have to learn and practice the Kegel or PC muscle sexercises in Chapter 8. They are easy to learn but require a conscious effort to practice regularly and to increase the pressure you use. There are some interesting toys and devices available to women who want to become good at this trick.

ALERT!

Make sure any stools, hassocks, or furniture you use won't slip out from under you. Placing them near a wall or the back of an overstuffed couch will help keep them in place.

Inverted Standing Positions

Positions such as the Wheelbarrow are healthy for the glandular system and are fun to try if you are careful. You'll need to be fairly physically fit to try these positions. Strong arms and legs are a must. Find ways to move into these positions as a natural adaptation from other, less strenuous ones.

The Wheelbarrow

In the Wheelbarrow Position the woman is on her hands only and has her head on the floor, a pillow, or free from support. The man is standing. He supports her by holding her legs and feet, in the air, while he enters her. Generally, the woman's legs would be at about his hips' height, much like a wheelbarrow's handles might be.

This position is very erotic to the man as he has a bird's-eye view of gorgeous buttocks and the pelvic freedom to thrust effortlessly. A variation on this theme is to have the woman resting on a hassock or footstool so that she is a little higher up in relationship to her partner. To get into this position more easily, you can start by using the "Congress of the Cow:" "When a woman stands on her hands and feet like a quadruped, and her lover mounts her like a bull, it is called: the Congress of the Cow" Part 2, Chapter 6, Sutra 37. The man can then pick up one or two of the woman's feet and lift her legs to hold them. There are shoulder supports for inversion postures in yoga that may add an interesting dimension to this position, too.

The Inverted Crow

The classic "69" oral sex position is the basis for this standing position variation. It may not be too difficult for a woman who is relatively small to try this position. She can hook her legs over the man's shoulders to help hold herself in position and use her hands on his knees for additional support. Some of the love furniture that is on the market might be useful for her to rest her head on in this position.

Chapter 13

Positions Inspired by Nature

Every ancient love book—from the Japanese Ishimpo, the Indian Ananga Ranga, to the Indian Kama Sutra—teaches about the importance of observing animals in nature and their sexual escapades. Indeed, many of the lovemaking notions of the Kama Sutra come from this observation. Love bites from lions, the notion of fluttering from butterflies, and the idea of spooning from snakes all have inspired past couples to try new positions.

Of Birds, Bees, Fish, and Lions

The ancient Kama Sutra texts talk about the physical health and psychological growth that can become available to you when you break away from your normal habits of lovemaking. When you move into nature, for example, you can mimic the birds and the bees, the lioness and her suitor, or two fish swimming side by side. By combining your human awareness with your animal-like nature, you and your lover can invent new positions that are fun and just right for you. You can also become more aware of each other when you remove yourselves from your usual surroundings.

The Kama Sutra suggests that the amorous couple mimic the sounds that the specific animals make when they are engaged in sex. Squeals, moans, grunts, chirps, roars, deep sighs, and purring allow the couple to forget about being intimidated so that they can expand and merge more easily.

Off to the Zoo

Go on an outing to the zoo with your lover or look at some National Geographic books. Check out how the animals have sex. The ancient Taoists, Native Americans, and Tantrics who studied manuscripts such as the Kama Sutra believed that animals had a lot to teach us about lovemaking and positions.

What do you see? Notice what the tigers are doing. The male will typically mount the female from the rear, hold her head down, and gently but aggressively bite her neck and pull her ruff. Lions, cheetahs, and most other cats make love this way, too.

This position allows for deep thrusting. The male is in more control than the female. The erotic stimulation to the back of the neck, earlobes, and even the hair and head add extra input to some of the more important erogenous zones. The female can move and lift her hips, but she cannot make large moves. The human female can subtly move to help create contact with her G-spot.

Monkeys sit facing each other for sex, but mostly they make love from the rear. They sit on their haunches, though. When humans try this position, they can modify it by having the man sit on his knees and the woman place herself sitting on top of him, facing the same direction. She has the added movement and use of her legs to help raise and lower her body in response to her partner. She can also move from side to side to add to the friction and G-spot access.

QUESTION?

How about the positions that snakes use?
The spooning positions would be analogous positions for these creatures. Try undulating together for that slinky feeling.

The Good-for-You Positions

Animals will often make love in positions that take the least amount of energy possible. This sets a good example, especially for people who may not be in the best of shape, healthwise. The positions that lions and tigers use are similar to the "Cat" yoga posture discussed in Chapter 17. It's easy on the hips and back.

The snake or spooning positions are good positions for freeing the hips and for reducing lower back pain, too. They are also good for men who have larger than average lingams. The thighs of the woman take up some of the man's lingam, giving a feeling of a tighter fit all around.

Making Love Outside

Go out in nature, and observe. Try your own mimicry. Swim like the fish and try undulating together underwater. No one can see you in a lake. Mimic the actions and the interactions of many different animals—even insects.

It's often difficult, in modern living situations, to get to an outdoor place that feels safe for expressing sexual love. If you have a private backyard, you can create beautiful gardens and areas where you can feel secure enough to have sex out-of-doors. Swimming pools and hot tubs are good but remember to use a water-based lubricant and make sure the water quality is good.

A porch swing or hammock, lawn furniture, the swimming pool, or even the lawn area next to a tree stump would work. You can set up a hook, for a purchased love-swing, in different places around the yard or in the house. All these things will add exciting new variations to your lovemaking.

◀ The Swing

Nature-Inspired Positions

With names like The Clinging Creeper, Crab Position, and Tortoise Position, don't you think you could have a little fun? Erotic couples of the past spent time in nature. They would closely observe the insects, animals, and birds to become inspired to create new positions for lovemaking.

The Crab Position

"When the woman's legs are bent at the knees and wedged below the man's navel just before congress, it is named the Crab Position" (Part 2, Chapter 6, Sutra 28). This position requires a good deal of yogic ability. You will have to be very limber to try this one. Small women will be able to get their toes on the pubic bone of their partner, just below the navel. The woman should hug her knees to her chest in this position.

ALERT!

Be very careful when trying anything new that may be a stretch for your physical body. Endorphins, those chemicals your body produces when you're having fun, can cover up pain. Playing now, and experiencing pain later, won't help you remember the fun part.

The Lotus Position

"When the thighs are crossed, so that the right foot is on the left thigh and the left foot is on the right thigh, it is named 'the Lotus Position'" (Part 2, Chapter 6, Sutra 30). The woman sits in a full Lotus Position, as if she were meditating, but she brings her legs toward her chest and holds them tightly. The man can either sit by her side or in front of her, or be on top of her.

The Clinging Creeper

"Her limbs, entwined in yours, like tendrils of fragrant jasmine creeper, draw taut and slowly relax in the gentle rhythm of lingam and yoni."

To get a graphic picture of how this is done, open up both of your hands, make the "scissors" shape with your first and second fingers on each hand and put them together to "cut" each other. The resulting shape would be the position that the two of you would assume. This position is comfortable and is good for relaxing and resting while loving. Women will find that one side or the other is best for them. See which suits you.

▲ The Clinging Creeper Position

Nature Postures from the Ananga Ranga

The variations on some of the "nature" postures are interesting, to say the least. The Ananga Ranga put the many positions it recognized into six appropriate categories. Here are a few of the selections to try:

- "If, seated face to face, your toes caress the lovely woman's nipples, her feet press your chest and you make love holding each other's hands it is The Tortoise."
- "Seated, the lady raises one foot to point vertically over her head and steadies it with her hands, offering up her "yoni" for lovemaking: this is The Peacock."
- "If, sitting facing her, you grasp her ankles and fasten them like a chain behind your neck, and she grips her toes as you make love, it is the delightful The Lotus."

- "The round-thighed woman on the bed grasps her ankles and raises high her lotus feet; you strike her to the root, kissing and slapping open-palmed between her breasts—this is The Monkey."
- "She cups and lifts her buttocks with her palms, spreads wide her thighs, and digs in her heels besides her hips, while you caress her breasts—this is The Flower in Bloom."
- "She draws her limbs together, clasping her knees tightly to her breasts, her yoni, like an opening bud, offered up for pleasure: this is known as The Bud."

In and Around the House

The home, both inside and out, gives many opportunities in which to experience new positions. The Kama Sutra has some positions you thought you'd probably never try, but most of them aren't really that hard. Trying some of them might involve a great deal of laughter or it might lead you to whole new discoveries for sexual satisfaction.

Spread a lush carpet or blanket in front of the fireplace. Bring as many pillows out as you can find. They'll give you a variety of options for shaping your environment to suit the positions you might want to try.

Furniture Positions

There are many opportunities inside the house to experiment with new positions. The kitchen table is often the perfect height for intercourse. Try the counter for oral sex. Have the woman bend over the arm of the overstuffed chair in the living room for rear entry. The woman can also sit on the arm of the sofa and have her partner kneel on the cushions as he enters her. This is a good position in which to put one of your feet up on the back of the couch. Choose the side of the couch that will best allow you freedom of movement and maximum G-spot access.

◀ A hassock is very useful for lovemaking.

Get yourselves a hassock. They are fantastic for the Modified Yab/Yum Position. The man sits on the hassock and his partner seats herself on top of him and closes her legs around him. He supports her back with his hands. This position is easy on his back. It gives both partners the freedom to rock, grind, and undulate to their hearts' content.

Swinging and Swaying

"Sitting face to face in bed, her breasts pressed tight against your chest, let each of you lock heels behind the other's waist, and lean back clasping one another's wrists. Now, set the swing gently in motion, your beloved, in pretended fear, clinging to your body with her flawless limbs, cooing and moaning with pleasure: this is The Swing." This is a more advanced position, as it requires a lot of mobility and strong stomach muscles. Don't lie all the way down—just lean back so that you can get the swing going that makes this position so unique.

"If, by means of some contraption, your lover suspends herself above you, places your lingam in her yoni and pulleys herself up and down upon it, it is called The Orissan." Love swings reappeared a few years back as a result of the new interest in the Kama Sutra. Old Kama Sutra paintings show couples making love on them.

A variety of positions can be played with, and best of all, one or both partners can be weightless in a swing. Sometimes the woman is in the swing and is positioned above the man who is reclining on the floor or bed. Sometimes they are in separate swings near each other. In the modern versions, you can even get in together. They are portable, fun, and versatile.

F A C T

There are only about twenty-four positions or postures in the whole Kama Sutra. Couples are left to explore variations to the themes on their own, as they mature in their ability to create pleasure for each other.

Swings promote relaxation and multiple orgasmic responses in both men and women. Men will most likely find them a good tool for learning and maintaining ejaculation control. Because they're so portable, you can hang them in strategic locations around your home and garden, and enjoy them anywhere.

Snakelike Spooning Positions

"Spooning" positions are a wonderful addition to any couple's repertoire of lovemaking. They are especially great for either the very beginning or the very end of a lovemaking session. Because these positions are greatly nurturing, partners can use them to connect deeply before making love, or they can use them at the very end, for holding and lying still in those magical moments before drifting off to sleep.

These positions can be used whether the man's penis is erect or not. Just holding each other in these positions has its place in any lovemaking situation. They can also be used when the two of you desire to make love but the woman is low on energy, or when both of you are more tired than usual and you want to stay very mellow. With the woman in front and the man behind holding her, the couple can gently undulate, whether having intercourse, or just bonding.

▲ A Snakelike Position

In the spoonlike position, you generally assume a position similar to spoons lying next to each other. Front to front or back to front with either the man or the woman in front, depending on who needs the most cuddling. Bring the arm and hand that is under you to the front, under the person in front, so that you can hold them near their heart area. The other hand can come over the top to hold their pelvis region close to yours. Pull them to you and snuggle up close.

Spoon positions allow the couple to move their pelvises freely. Undulating in these positions is particularly sensual and erotic. Use this variety of position for pairings in which the man has a very large lingam and the woman is on the smaller side. When he is behind her, her thighs create more friction for the man's pleasure when he is inside of her and she won't be as vulnerable to being hurt.

The Crow or "69" Position

"If the pair of you lie side by side, facing opposite ways, and kiss each other's secret parts, it is known as The Crow" (Part 2, Chapter 9, Sutra 34).

This is the classic "69" position that is very well known in contemporary society. It is one of the few positions in the Kama Sutra that isn't actually a position of intercourse. Nevertheless, it is named as a position. When two women are in this position, it is called "The Gobbling of the Fishes."

Sometimes the Crow isn't a perfect fit, though. If the partners are very different in height, it can be difficult to reach each other's genitals. In the case of male-female lovers, the woman often ends up being a bit more active because of the exterior nature of the man's genitals. It is more conducive to orgasm to have the mouth free for deep breathing during love play. This isn't possible in the 69 position because both lovers are "giving" and their mouths are busy.

> The Crow is the only way that partners can engage in oral sex at the same time. Both get stimulated simultaneously. Either lover can be on top. It's an easy position to flip over in for variety.

Men often like faster, harder stimulation than women. When a couple falls in sync during lovemaking, the man may be leading and this can cause the woman to feel like she's not getting the kind of stimulation she likes. They may need to slow down and focus on her a little more. Use your nails to lightly scratch and your mouth to lightly bite. Use sound to add to the variety. Growl and howl, groan and whimper, moan and hum!

▲ The Crow ("69") Position

The Clasping Position

"When, during actual congress, the legs of both the lovers are straightened and stretched, it is called the Clasping Position" (Part 2, Chapter 6, Sutra 16). This position can be done with the partners facing each other sideways, or with the man on top of the woman. It's a quiet position that is restful and refreshing. It is the position a couple would be in before moving into the Twinning Position.

The Twinning Position

"'The twinning position' results when, in 'the clasping position', the woman turns her left thigh to the right and the right one to the left. The mutual turning of the thigh contracts the abdomen even more than in other positions" (Part 2, Chapter 6, Sutra 19). Literally, the woman wraps one of her legs around the thigh of her lover—either side will do. This allows for deeper penetration and movement, especially on the part of the woman.

ALERT!

It's hard for some people to focus on receiving attention while they are giving attention. The Crow or 69 Position is an example of this. Be aware that this may be a position you will want to explore, but it may not work for both of you to have orgasms in.

Theme Variations

In the many ancient love manuals from Asian cultures around the globe, it rarely seems as though you'll see a position duplicated. There are literally hundreds of variations to the multitude of positions. Slight, subtle changes and movements often create a completely different experience than the one just before it. "These postures for congress can be equally well employed in water as well as the ground—in lying down, sitting, or standing attitudes" (Part 2, Chapter 6, Sutra 32).

Then, there are as many variations on couples and partners as there are words in all the languages of the world. Experiment with a shift of a leg or even a foot. A hand under a buttocks or a leg over one shoulder can give a shift to the angle of the lingam in the yoni. One such change may be all that is needed for the woman to be able to orgasm through intercourse.

Changing positions often during lovemaking could be the difference for a man who wants to delay ejaculation so that he can maintain the high states of arousal necessary to have several orgasmic peaks. He will discover creative ways to manage his sexual energy so that he can pleasure his partner for as long as she likes. Positions that offer variety will help him pace himself in the dance of love.

Let Your Imagination Go Wild

Sometimes it's hard to let go during sex. The more you try new things with your partner, though, the more easily you'll be able to let go into the fun and pleasure. Don't worry about whether something seems "right" or not. Try it anyway. You'll soon find out. Imagination is something you have to stretch to make it work smoothly.

Let your imagination go wild! Have sex on the warm hood of your station wagon out in the country. Pitch a tent in your living room, during the winter, and decorate it as if it were a sultan's tent. Make love on the nest of pillows you put inside. Try some new positions in the swimming pool or the hot tub. Take turns thinking up new places and ways to make love.

It's difficult to let go of the day-to-day world sometimes when you're having sex. Did you finish this, did the kids do that, are they asleep, am I hard enough, are my thighs wobbling—the worries can go on and on. By remembering to breathe deeply and focusing back on your pleasurable feelings, you can quickly bring yourself back to the moment.

Keep in mind that you are taking each other on an erotic journey whether you are making love as usual or trying a new fun position. Draw your partner in by keeping close contact with soft, intimate eyes. Study each other's facial expressions. Stay very connected and remember to breathe deeply. Get creative and experiment. You've nothing to lose and a whole lot of fun to gain! Ⓔ

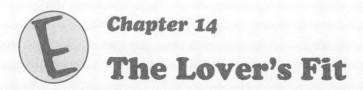

Chapter 14
The Lover's Fit

Ah, the dance of the sexes. When it works, it works well but you can't always take this for granted, especially in a new relationship. How do you know that you will be compatible? What do you do if you're not? When you've got the mix of emotions, character, body dimensions, experience, and even cultural and religious beliefs, how do you understand and work with what the two of you bring to the union?

The Temperaments of Men and Women

The ancient Taoist philosophers from China taught that a woman's energy comes from the heavens and moves down through her body, and that a man's energy moves from the earth and up through his body. This is a veiled way of saying that women want love and heart connection first, and then they will warm up to the idea of sexual activity. Men, on the other hand, want sexual activity first, and then they will warm up to love and heart connection. This single idea provides a summation for what many couples feel they experience about each other's temperaments in sexual partnerships.

Yin and Yang

The sexual war of the sexes: She needs heart connection before she wants to have sexual connection, whereas he needs sex before he wants to have heart connection. You have seen the symbol of the yin/yang circle with the light and the dark intersecting halves that curl around each other. This symbol is a representation of both the masculine energy (yang energy) and the feminine energy (yin energy). In the big picture, the symbol also represents the world or the individual and the balance that might be sought in those realms, too.

Understanding that these oppositions exist in each of us and that the world is constructed this way helps to calm the fears and move us forward in finding new ways to love. Learning new positions is one of the best ways to deconstruct the anomaly of opposites. Your choice of positions can have a major influence on your yin/yang relationship.

Living in this world you encounter sadness, violence, hurt, and what modern psychologists call the "shadow." It is present in each of our individual lives. You have your parts that you feel safer hiding from a person close to you, and on the other hand you have the great parts that you are proud of and want to share. This is called the "light" and can be seen in people everywhere when they are generous, compassionate, and loving toward others around them.

Proceeding in the Face of Opposites

Yin is Taoist for the feminine or receptive principle. Yang is the male or active principle. The position you choose, and its appropriateness for your particular needs, can make the difference in whether you experience a female-male "energy dance" or a "war of the sexes." When a woman opens up her sexual repertoire to include trying positions where she is on top and in control, she becomes the "male" principle, or the yang one in the sex act at that moment. This empowers her, and can give her a growing confidence in taking a more sexually active role.

When the male is on the bottom, he can move into his more yin, or feminine, side. This takes the heat off, so to speak. He can relax. He doesn't have to be in charge and perform. The simple act of trying a new position can often be transformative for a relationship.

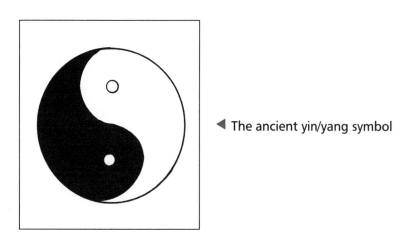

◀ The ancient yin/yang symbol

Yin/Yang in Everyday Life

Moving these principles forward to extend into our everyday actions can be challenging for some people. The woman who refuses to check her own car's oil, help plant the family garden, drive the car while going somewhere with her man, or explore understanding of the household plumbing is not a very integrated person. If she is caught up in how she looks at all times and portrays herself as the helpless, incapable feminine woman, she will draw a man who embodies her opposite. She will then complain bitterly that he doesn't listen, can't "feel," and is insensitive. They are holding opposite poles for each other and neither of them will have an easy time breaking the codependence of the relationship.

ALERT!

Without having the stressful push to become a "superwoman" or a "superman," learn to say yes to a variety of experiences and responsibilities in life. Look to see if something you are being asked to do is an opportunity to expand who you are in ways that may be a little challenging.

For men, the male force you must surmount is the one to be the leader, the "doer," the macho man, and the action figure. The key, for instance, in learning to have multiple orgasmic peaks is to completely relax while in high states of arousal. This is a very "yin" or feminine energy. Being vulnerable to the idea of not knowing everything or having all the answers is a valuable position to be in. Practice by letting your intuition lead sometimes is a wonderful lesson in expanding a more "feminine" perspective.

The Kinds of Physical Unions

The Kama Sutra divides men and women into several distinctive categories depending on the size of the genitals, the nature of the desire of the individual, their timing, and the shape of their genitals. As you can imagine it gets to be quite a science to determine exactly who you are in this milieu of combinations. These categories and combinations may help you if you are in either extreme end of the spectrum. Otherwise, it may be wise to read them purely for the erotic knowledge.

Genital Categories

Yoni and lingam sizes are said to be of three kinds with a total of nine combinations possible for intercourse. Man is divided into three classes: the Hare Man, the Bull Man, and the Horse Man, according to the size of his lingam. Woman also, according to the depth of her yoni, is either a female deer, a mare, or a female elephant.

The Kama Sutra describes these various types as such:

- The Hare Man is a lively individual with a slight body type and a gentle manner. His lingam is considered to be of the small variety and measures about six finger widths in length, which is equivalent to about 4 inches.
- The Bull Man has a sturdy body and holds himself with esteem. He is considered of a medium size and his temperament is hearty and energetic. When erect, he measures about eight finger widths, or 5½ inches.
- The Stallion, or Horse Man, is the largest of the three. He is said to be tall and muscular and has a sense of adventurism and daring. He measures twelve finger widths, which equals about 8 inches.
- The Deer Woman is the smallest of the types of women. She's of slight build, is gentle, and it is said that her secretions smell like a new lotus blossom opening. Her yoni is narrow and not very deep, thus she is best pared with the Hare Man.
- The Mare Woman has a medium-size yoni. She is said to be sturdy in body, and conducts life with a flare. Her personality is positive and sensuous. She is best suited to partner with a Bull Man, and her vulva area is full and generous.
- The Elephant Woman is large boned and often has a taller-than-average body. She is affable and agreeable and can have a rather ruddy complexion. She is best partnered with a Stallion Man as he can bring her deep yoni the most pleasure.

Expanding Ancient Beliefs

Though these categories are rather simplistic, they do point out that humans can vary tremendously in their features. It is more obvious that men differ in the size of their genitals than women, as their genitals are mostly hidden. The largest percentage of men and women fall into the center category, though, with exceptions on either side.

FACT

In a survey of 2,400 people on the tantra.com Web site, fewer than 29 percent said they liked their body size and shape. Cultural images of skinny models and big muscles tend to lead us astray in understanding that our bodies work well for us when we put aside our self-talk and come fully to the present moment in our sexual activities.

Though it seems rational and wise advice to pick a partner who fits your size, you can't tell your mind who to fall in love with. There will always be those lovers who may not have the perfect fit. With creative attention to the variety of positions that can be used to shape your experience, there need not be any "low" unions, as Vatsyayana called the imperfect fit.

The G-spot is only about 1½ inches inside of the yoni. If both partners are in good health and the woman has kept her PC or vaginal muscles in strong shape, the size of the partner's genitals isn't really of concern. A variety of great sexual positions can create the best connections when both the man and woman understand their bodies and know the very best ways to guarantee a pleasurable experience.

Lingam Shapes

In addition to size, ancient texts examine the distinct shapes of a man's lingam. These shapes have nothing to do with size. Again, three categories are sighted:

- A penis with the head and shaft of the same dimensions in width.
- A penis with the shaft thicker than the head.
- A penis with the head thicker around than the shaft.

The penis with the head thicker around than the shaft is said to be the best shape for friction to the G-spot in the woman, hence the most pleasure. The frenulum catches on the G-spot with every stroke out and puts a maximum amount of pressure in this area. Positions in which the woman puts her legs back against her body and in high positions on her partner's shoulders can create the same pressure and friction.

Approximately 80 percent of men have penises that are "average" size: this means between 5 and 7 inches in length with the most common being 6 to 6½ inches. Girth is commonly between 4½ and 5½ inches.

The Kinds of Emotional Unions

The scholars who wrote the sutras were also interested in the duration in timing and the passion that each individual might bring to a sexual encounter. They understood that there are many types of people—some more passionate than others, others more intense or thinking types. Calm, nervous, or aggressive—there are matches for everyone and lovemaking styles to suit all types.

"A man is considered to have small passion when he has little desire for union with a woman, who does not exert himself much at the time, and whose flow is scanty. He also evades the woman's teeth marks. When a man has some force of passion, he belongs to the second class and if his passion is very strong, he qualifies for the third, intense class" (Part 2, Chapter 1, Sutras 13–14). "Similarly, women are reckoned to have the three varying degrees of passion, and nine different combinations, exactly like those based on dimensions" (Part 2, Chapter 1, Sutras 15–16).

Timing Temperaments

Timing in sexual activity means that one man may take a lot longer to get aroused than another man—as it is with women. There is a misconception that men are always ready for sex. This isn't true. In addition, both men and women go through periods in their lives when they have a fluctuation of sexual desire. Job stress, family obligations, and life pressures can put an undue amount of constraint on the most balanced of people causing their passionate pursuits to wane. This is natural and to be expected.

"Again, there are three types of men and women according to their individual passions—short timed, medium timed, and long timed, and there are nine combinations of possible unions, as before" (Part 2, Chapter 1, Sutra 17). There is disagreement though when the discussion turns to the pleasure derived from sexual activity. "The woman does not discharge the same way as the man. While the man, by merely uniting with the woman, is able to fulfill his passion, the woman takes pleasure in the consciousness of desire and this gives her the kind of pleasure that is totally different from the man's" (Part 2, Chapter 1, Sutras 19–22).

The passage implies that women have a kind of spiritual orgasm but not a real, physical one. This is obviously not true and in other areas of the Kama Sutra it is countered with the idea that women do "emit" like men and, in fact, do orgasm distinctly. It further suggests that women do not like men who are of the short-timed variety because they do not feel satisfied when making love to them. They ejaculate too early.

◀ Create timing that works for both of you.

Learn Your Sexual Nature

Modern doctors and psychologists understand that men and women cover the full spectrum along the lines of timing. If partners are patient and are both willing to learn more about their own partner's needs and issues, as well as their own, there are no reasons this should be an issue with lovers.

Sometimes psychological, organic, or physical issues can keep men and women from being orgasmic at all or ejaculating too fast. Don't hesitate to see your doctor if these kinds of things are causing problems in your life. Do learn new things about your own sexual nature and grow by applying and trying these new things. Relax, let go, and expand your sexual and sensual attitudes.

Practice keeping your eyes soft and open during the many different situations you encounter in your day. If you can do it during sex, you will be a lot more comfortable with this practice in the rest of the situations you find yourself in.

Body Characteristics and Genital Size

The Chinese Taoists developed involved theories about body parts, and even posture as it might pertain to genital size and sexual temperament. These theories developed over thousands of years and so may be considered at least somewhat accurate. Though none of us would go around searching the thumb shape or eye structure in order to find a prospective mate, it's an interesting study in possibilities.

Marriage Partners in Ancient Times

In the days when parents and matchmakers found marriage partners for their children, it was important to choose robust and good sexual matches. People were very concerned with continuing their lineages, producing grandchildren, and honoring their ancestors. Matches were made when the two to be married were very young, and so facial and body structure, as well as feet and hand structure became important factors in choosing partners.

◀ Body characteristics make interesting study.

Facial Characteristics

Some of the interesting conclusions include eye structure patterns that can indicate certain types of people. People with large eyes tend to be great lovers. Small eyes indicate a rational, straight-thinking personality type. Men with large eyes are expert lovers, whereas women with large eyes are more open and willing.

Most cultures believe that the eyes are the windows to the soul. That is why it is important to leave a soft light on while making love and to practice keeping your eyes open during sexual activity. Witnessing your lover and having him or her witness you creates an intimate bubble that surrounds the couple and keeps them completely connected.

The Taoists believed that abundant facial and body hair means that you have a deep sexual appetite. Thick eyebrows equal thick pubic hair, which was very desirable. Full, long eyebrows on a man indicate a long, robust penis.

Full, fleshy earlobes and large ears predict a strong sexual appetite. Long noses in men indicate long, strong lingams. Small, flat noses in women indicate a warm personality and a short, wide vaginal canal. If the nose of the woman is long, it predicts a sexually aggressive woman with an abundance of energy.

QUESTION?

What is your sexual profile?
Look at the categories in this chapter and rate yourself by making a simple list of the qualities that you see in yourself. If you are partnered, ask your lover to do the same. If you see some areas where you believe you may not quite mesh, list some creative ideas to help you expand your lovemaking in those areas.

Hand Characteristics

The Taoists constructed a detailed analysis of the structure of the hands and fingers for predicting the size of men's and women's genitals. They believed that long, straight fingers, especially the first finger, indicated a long penis. In contrast, short, stocky fingers indicated a thick penis. A thumb that is narrow at the base where it meets the hand but wide at the tip means that this man possesses a penis with a head that is larger than the shaft. This is a good sign for a great lover.

Women with straight fingers have a wide vaginal opening and a wide interior vagina. If their thumbs are narrow at the base near the hand and wide at the tip, then the entrance to the vagina is narrow and the interior is wide. Short fingers indicate a short, narrow vaginal canal.

Creating the Perfect Fit

Sometimes a couple won't have the best possible fit with their body parts for sex. A woman might have a large vagina, while her partner has a smaller penis. You might envy a man with a large penis, but he will often complain that lovers leave him because he hurts them. Through exploring new techniques that expand both intercourse and nonintercourse stimulation, and by studying ancient books such as the Kama Sutra, these obstacles are easily overcome.

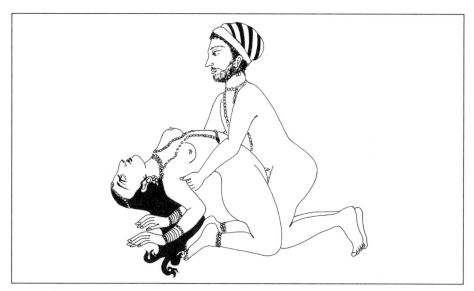

▲ Make a perfect fit by getting creative.

Experiment with New Positions

Any couple experiencing these and other "fit" problems should experiment with new positions to get the very best out of their lovemaking. Positions that hurt the woman or don't allow her to move her hips and adjust her body to her partner's are going to contribute to an uncomfortable sexual experience. If the woman or man can't communicate problems like this, the couple may begin to shy away from sexual activity.

This can be the beginning of a downhill spiral in the relationship. The couple may never come out of it, all because neither person could say that he or she wasn't comfortable with the way their sexual experiences were going. Exploring new positions can help.

Positions for Large Couples

Your willingness to remain supple in your body and to maintain a fun attitude goes a long way in creating new experiences for you as partners. Remember that your body is your temple, so don't get stopped by issues such as size and shape. Each position can be played with, experimented with, added to, and explored by any size couple, but these suggestions work well for larger couples.

The positions that might best suit you are the rear entry, modified Yab/Yum, woman on top, and a kind of scissors form. One key is to have a lot of varied-size pillows around the bed so that you are perfectly comfortable with some of these modifications. You may even want to try a love-swing to create a feeling of weightlessness.

Rear-Entry Positions

Rear-entry positions are unique in that the woman is facing away from her partner. This keeps your tummies from competing for space. The woman can either be on hands and knees with the man behind, or she can be in this same position but the man is standing. This gives both of you maximum leeway to move around. This is also an excellent G-spot position, and in general, standing increases the strength of the man's erection. I highly suggest a hand mirror for the woman to hold so that the two of you can eye gaze while making love.

Modified Yab/Yum Position

The Modified Yab/Yum Position is when the man sits on a fairly firm surface with his legs out and slightly apart. His partner sits on him with a firm pillow under her buttocks. She can lean back slightly against a wall or headboard as a variation. This would increase the friction on her G-spot.

Experiment, experiment, experiment—try new positions, use pillows and love furniture, create scenarios that appeal to your imaginations, tease and titillate each other, and get away to other locations. In other words—play at sex! Childlike innocence can serve you well in the bedroom.

Woman-Superior Positions

In the woman-superior positions, if the woman stays upright and doesn't lean toward her partner too much, their tummies won't get in the way and, again, this is a great G-spot position. If it is appropriate, hang a bar or rod from the ceiling that the woman can hold on to during lovemaking to lift herself up and down with. This creates easier thrusting, and it's fun and exciting to consider. You can take it down when not in use.

The Twinning Branches

The Twinning Branches is an easy position that can be relaxing, too. It is easiest to describe by using your hands to first create the concept with. Open up the fingers on both of your hands, make the "scissors" shape with your first and second fingers on each hand, and put them together to "cut" each other. The resulting shape would be the position that the two of you would assume. This position is comfortable and restful and is easily adjusted to get the best fit for both of you.

Positions for Mismatched Couples

Many people are involved in relationships where one of the members is very much taller than the other. This is usually the man but not always. Some sexual positions just won't work very well for these couples because they can't get near enough to each other. According to the Taoists, the tall man may also have quite big genitals, while the woman may have smaller-than-average depth to her yoni.

Again, pillows and love furniture can be helpful to these couples. Beanbag chairs, hassocks, love swings, stuffed sofa arms, and large pillows can add the dimension of adventure and help with bodily discrepancies. If you are athletically inclined, try some of the standing postures or positions detailed in Chapter 12.

All women, whether of the Deer type, the Mare type, or the Elephant type, should be practicing their PC muscle or Kegel exercises. You will increase your sexual desire, your focus, your orgasmic potential, and you will pleasure yourself and your partner more effectively.

Tall men can place their partners on the kitchen counter with a pillow under her buttocks. A bar stool works well, also. This height may be perfect and if she hangs her legs over your arms at the elbow, you may be able to pick her up for a standing position.

Spoon positions work well for couples where his lingam is very large and she has a hard time accommodating its full length. By holding her legs close together during intercourse, the woman can add friction to her partner's penis and also protect herself from thrusting that is too deep. This is especially important to remember because the G-spot is only a little way into the woman, so for her to be sexually aroused he may need to do some thrusting patterns with some shallow thrusts and then some deeper thrusts.

When a couple is partnered where the woman has a generous yoni and the man may be more of the Hare-type man or even the Bull-type man, the couple should use positions that allow the woman to open her legs very freely. She should also try to stay limber enough to be able to put her legs up onto her partner's shoulders to increase the angle of penetration. This causes the penis to enter the vagina at a more oblique angle. This adds much more friction to the encounter. (E)

Chapter 15

Orgasm Mastery

The Kama Sutra illustrates many different positions, ways of being partnered, the arts one should study, and a myriad of other prescriptions for a good sex life, but it doesn't teach exactly how to experience orgasm. It is particularly remiss when it comes to women. Time and focus is needed for orgasm mastery, but the knowledge of the genitals and each individual's sexual response curve is especially important.

Orgasm Variety

The understanding and care that a woman might require to reach the orgasmic state may not have been understood by some men in the Kama Sutra's culture. When you read the passage below, it appears that this particular scholar was unaware of what an orgasm was like in women. It actually appears as though the women might not have known either or, at least, didn't express themselves.

"Females do not emit as males do. The males simply remove their desire, while the females, from their consciousness of desire, feel a certain kind of pleasure, which gives them satisfaction, but it is impossible for them to tell you what kind of pleasure they feel. The fact from which this becomes evident is, that males, when engaged in coition, cease of themselves after emission, and are satisfied, but it is not so with females." —Auddalika, an ancient scholar, in response to a passage in Part 3, Chapter 1 of the Kama Sutra

This passage proves that women are either multiorgasmic and actually crave repeat orgasms or, as is the case with some women, don't know what orgasm is. Yes, pleasure is felt, but the actual release to the point of vaginal and uterine contractions isn't experienced. When they finally have a true orgasm, the gates are opened for the recognition of the actual experience.

Orgasm, in both men and women, varies from person to person and from moment to moment. The same person might recognize that she has a variety of experiences depending on mood, situation, timing, place, stress, and more. The more experience and expansive understanding that you have, the more consistent your pleasure will be.

The Clitoral Orgasm

Long heralded as "the only avenue to female orgasm," the clitoris has always been known as the woman's pleasure center. The clitoris has the largest bundle of nerve endings of any organ in the body, male or female. It stays active from birth to death and is as much a source of pleasure as it is frustration.

Know Thyself

The clitoris is located on the outside of the woman's body toward the top of her vulva—the opening to her vagina. The same tissue that makes up the sides of the vulva and the labia covers the clitoris with a hood of skin. The hood extends over the clitoris and generally covers it to protect it from overstimulation.

In the past, many young women have been encouraged not to touch themselves, or explore their genital area. They may have been shamed, discouraged, and even threatened by an authority figure in their life. As a result, these women didn't give themselves permission to self-pleasure or at least explore their "Sacred Garden" until later in life.

Orgasms can feel brief, expansive, deep, short, extended, mild, earthshaking, odd, and any other variety of adjectives you might want to ascribe to them. Strong ones can come when you least expect them, or when you do expect them, they can be "blips." Unless you are well trained in the matters of love, you just never know what you are going to get.

Many women still don't feel comfortable touching themselves, let alone receiving the full pleasure that is their birthright. No wonder that they struggle or at least feel frustration when it comes to orgasmic pleasure. But you must know what pleases you (pressure, stroke, etc.) and how to facilitate an orgasm in yourself.

Building a Wave of Pleasure

When the clitoris is stimulated, it begins to fill with a surge of blood, much like the penis. The spongy material around the nerve bundle fills and causes the clitoris to actually become erect. As this happens, the clitoris enlarges slightly and you become more aroused. If you are getting the kind of stimulus you like, you should continue the build of excitement toward an orgasm.

However, often at the point of around 8—on an arousal scale of 1 to 10—the woman will have a variety of experiences that will prevent her from continuing the climb toward orgasm. She may tense her body excessively, she may stop breathing altogether, or she may begin to worry that she's taking too long—any number of both physical and mental bad habits may creep into her experience to put a damper on her pleasure.

Learning to relax and deep breathe into the belly will help tremendously. Focusing your mind on your pleasure sensations is a wonderful way to learn a kind of meditation technique. Learning to break down the barriers that prevent you from communicating what you need to your partner will greatly enhance both of your experiences.

This focused attention will also allow you to develop a kind of wave of sensations that you can trust and ride all the way to orgasm. There may be hills and valleys, but there are no ravines to fall into. As you master this wave, you will get better at knowing your body's responses and how to respond to them.

ALERT!

Becoming conscious of the minute details of your orgasmic potential seems like a selfish thing, but the opposite is true. When you become good at managing and receiving your own pleasure, you will want sex much more. It will be satisfying and rejuvenating. This is a journey with a goal for both of you to travel.

Clitoral Advice

In erotic love manuals of the East, including the Kama Sutra, the hand position that is often referred to for stimulating the woman's clitoris is called "Angulirata." It is described as using the first three fingers on the hand together to form a kind of an elephant's trunk shape. Put your fingers together such that if you look down at the three fingertips of your fingers you'll notice that they form a triangle. Your middle finger is positioned on top of the two other fingers that are close together but not quite touching.

By forming the fingers in this configuration, it is possible to anchor the clitoral shaft and stimulate the head and tip of the clitoris. The clitoris's nerve bundle can be elusive and a bit wiggly. By anchoring the shaft, you can keep it stationary, and massage and stimulate it appropriately. The two outside fingers anchor it and the middle finger stimulates.

The G-Spot and Vaginal Orgasm

According to most books on sex, there are two places in a woman's body that (when stimulated) can lead to an orgasm. The first is called the G-spot, but where it is and what it feels like are questions many women, and men, find unanswered. The second area is found in the vagina, back near the cervix opening and on top. It is a misconception that the vagina is a sensitive organ. It doesn't actually have many nerve endings, and other than the entrance—which has some sensitivity—these two areas are what you have to work with.

Location

Here's a little exercise: Place the tip of your tongue at the back of your front teeth, just touching the teeth. Move your tongue very slowly backward until you feel the ridge area that is rough and bumpy. As you slip past that area, you'll notice that the roof of your mouth begins to feel slick and smooth. You've gone too far.

Go back, with the very tip of your tongue, and find the place where these two meet. Just as the rough area ends, hold the tip there for a minute and place your conscious mind there, too. That place is exactly analogous to the area where the G-spot is in your yoni. The yoni is even shaped similarly to your upper palate. Try doing this same exercise with your thumb or finger in your mouth. Have your partner do it, too, in his or her mouth.

The G-spot is located right behind the pubic bone, just past the rough and ridge-like area on top of the vagina. It isn't very far in, about 1½ inches in most women and it is more of an area than a spot. It may burn, hurt a little, feel intense, feel great, or even tickle when you first realize it is there.

What to Do with It

If you think that you have located something in this area that feels a little different, great. Now, get turned on. Stimulate your clitoris, with or without a partner, to the point of about an 8 on the Richter scale. You will have an easier time actually finding your G-spot if you are turned on.

If you are stimulating yourself, a good position is to be on your knees so that you can reach your spot. Lying on your back will make it more difficult. Use the middle finger of your dominant hand to feel the area of the G-spot. Press quite firmly—you will be surprised how much pressure it takes. Use a come-hither motion of your finger to stroke the area.

If your partner is there with you, it is best to lie down with your legs bent at the knees and supported by pillows on either side. Your partner can sit to one side of you so that his or her dominant hand is free to enter your yoni. Partners, please pay very close attention to your lover. This is a vulnerable activity, especially if you are new to it. Keep eye contact with your lover.

FACT

A survey by Carol Rinkleib Ellison in her book *Women's Sexualities* found that 38 percent of 2,600 women studied had not once had an orgasm during intercourse. If this is you, you are not alone.

Once inside, try moving your finger slowly from side to side, like a windshield wiper. Then try the come-hither stroke. The "giver" can ask for feedback and the "receiver" should give quality feedback to the lover. Tell your partner what feels good and what doesn't. Tell what sensations you are having and any emotions that might be welling up.

Partners can remind each other to deep breathe during this exploration. Even the "giver" forgets to breathe sometimes. Relax and don't do too much exploration the first time. Make a commitment to try again soon and that time you can go a little longer. Build up to more intense pressure and speed slowly. Trust that you will discover the deep pleasure of this area.

Intercourse and the G-Spot

As you practice exploring this area with your fingers (and your lover's fingers), hold the image of it in your mind. You can do this a lot easier if you are practicing your PC muscle exercises. Strong vaginal muscles help you focus your attention on different areas of your vagina. Visualize your G-spot with your mind.

During intercourse have your partner do some shallow thrusting so that the head of his lingam just brushes the vaginal lips and the inside of your yoni. The stroke on the way out is often the most effective. Try this in positions in which the woman has her legs up high, say on her lover's shoulders. The angle of penetration will be conducive to G-spot stimulation. Try different positions to see which seem best for you.

Female Ejaculation

Yes, it's true, women ejaculate. It typically doesn't come in cups but in about the same amount as a man's ejaculate. It can pulse out, squirt out, dribble out, or come in little pulses. The women who recognize that they ejaculate tend to have strong vaginal muscles, good deep-breathing techniques, and often make deep sounds when they are in ecstasy.

Many women have been embarrassed that they "wet the bed" during sex and have done everything in their power to try to prevent it from occurring. We now know that women ejaculate and it has become something that women want to do. Don't push yourself to learn to ejaculate, though. It can be freeing, but it doesn't necessarily add to the orgasmic experience.

During G-spot play, you may want to try really opening up your vocal cords and letting out deep, resonate sounds and moans from your mouth. Play with the sounds freely to see what happens. Try it some time when the kids aren't home. Don't worry too much about the neighbors.

There are a few good videotapes on female ejaculation if you really want to explore it further. Be prepared with a thick towel and a willing spirit. You will feel the urge to pee but that is just your urethra being stimulated near the entrance of your vagina. It doesn't mean you are going to urinate. Sometimes a little urine is pushed out from the bladder during ejaculation so before trying this, go to the bathroom and make sure you have emptied your bladder.

Your partner isn't responsible for your orgasmic pleasure—you are. It is your responsibility to know what you need and to ask for it appropriately. Don't blame your lover if you are not getting the proper stimulation that you need to have orgasm pleasure.

The Male Orgasm

Women think that men just seem to come equipped with all the right gear and responses to have orgasms easily and effortlessly. Because their parts are so external most men have had a long history of self-loving activities. They know what brings them pleasure and are practiced at receiving it. The downside is they can be a little too good at it.

Myth has it that men are always ready for sex. Their penises get hard at the drop of a hat and they can have orgasms with no problems at all—all the time. If you are a man, you know better. Many obstacles can get in the way of orgasm and ejaculation. Yet most men enjoy the pleasures that orgasmic release brings with only a few off times throughout the years of their lives.

Early Training

Young men tend to masturbate, or self-pleasure, a lot more than young girls. Usually, young men train themselves to ejaculate quickly. This happens because of guilty feelings or the thought that they might get caught. Many Western societies tend to frown upon masturbation in both sexes.

As they get older, young men aren't taught that there are other ways to manage their sexual energy and the orgasmic reflex. If you are lucky enough, you will begin to realize that you don't have to "cum" as quickly as possible, and that if you don't, you will be bringing a lot more pleasure to your partner. Unfortunately, it may take a complaint or two from a woman to make a man take notice.

Being a Great Lover

Most men want to be great at loving. Sex is important to them and they have a vested interest in being considered good at it. By the time a man reaches his childbearing years, he often begins to slow his timing down to accommodate his lover. He'll learn that it's all right to take his time and really enjoy the sensations of sexual and sensual touch.

Lovers and partners tend to go on the journey together to learn and expand what they know about sex. This deepening can lead to some pretty extraordinary experiences that will reinforce the commitment to excel at sex and the intimate connection it brings. This is what brought ancient scholars, like Vatsyayana, to write books on this subject. Knowledge and the subtleties that come with experience can add up to unimaginable pleasure.

ALERT!

Smoking cigarettes and drinking excessive amounts of alcohol are the number-one killers of erections. Because the penis is far from the heart, it takes extra work for the blood to get there. These activities clog the arteries that supply the necessary blood flow to the penis.

Inhibitors to Good Sex

As both men and women get older, their blood flow gets more sluggish because the arteries begin to narrow. The blood flow to the penis decreases and becomes sluggish, also. At the same time, the veins that carry the blood back out of the penis begin to lose their elasticity and leak blood back out at the most inappropriate times.

It's important to keep having sex. The sex act counteracts the actions of normal aging. "Use it or lose it" is an active principle here. Men who practice even a marginal amount of ejaculation control have stronger, longer erections, too.

Take your vitamins and supplements. Try L-arginine as it opens arteries and increases blood flow. If you are on prescription medications that already do this, then try a topical cream that has the same effect. There are also creams that can have a very similar effect to Viagra for many men. The same creams are also available for women. However, make sure they have L-arginine in them.

Ejaculation Mastery for Men

Ejaculation mastery has been practiced in Asia for thousands of years. It is attributed to bringing a long healthy life and wise ways to the man who masters his "seed." Any man in ancient Asia who was wealthy enough to have a harem knew that he needed to satisfy all of his wives, or he would face their wrath!

It's All About Training

The basics of ejaculation control are simple, easy techniques that will help you to learn to last longer. That is your mission—to learn to retrain your sexual response. Training in any sport or activity that you want to be good at requires a bit of self-regulation. It requires a little discipline and time to acquire the knowledge to take the steps to mastery. Should you choose to accept this mission, it will require:

- Some quality time devoted to having fun training sessions
- Learning to relax in high states of arousal
- Changing your breathing habits from chest breathing to belly breathing
- Learning simple communication styles with your partner
- Loving your body and all the wonderful things it's capable of

Most men see significant results in just two weeks of practice. This might encompass six focused workouts. Sounds painful, doesn't it? You, and your partner if you have one, are about to embark on a wonderfully fulfilling journey that is remarkably easy for a significant number of men. While some men need to see a specialist, whether it is a psychologist or a urologist, for problems related to premature ejaculation, most men will be able to see good results from these simple steps.

The basic premise of learning ejaculation control is to practice solo or with a partner to simply last longer. This should begin with self-pleasuring that, on a scale of 1 to 10, stops every time you reach an 8 or 9. When you stop, relax and deep breathe into your belly for a few minutes and then start again. You need to relax your body completely.

The two biggest complaints men have about their sex lives are that they think their penis is too small and that they ejaculate too fast. Penis size has very little to do with being a good lover if the man knows what he is doing. Learning ejaculation mastery is fun and pretty easy for most men to accomplish in a very short time!

This will require some self-restraint at first. Bring your focus and willpower to bear. You'll soon understand that as you get closer to the ability to not go over the top you will actually be experiencing orgasmic-like pleasure without ejaculating.

Riding the Wave of Pleasure

Orgasmic-like pleasure will occur in peaks or waves of energy that you will begin to be able to ride like a surfer rides an ocean wave. The surfer gets up on top of the wave and stays there, subtly cutting back and forth to stay just ahead of the break, until he sees the shore coming. He gently cuts back out of the wave to avoid crashing, and easily paddles out for another ride. If he gets too far out in front of the wave, he goes over the top and the ride ends.

As you practice, you'll notice that you can get closer and closer to that "10 mark" without losing control. Your mind will be working with your body to recognize the point of no return sooner and sooner. Your ability to feel pleasure longer and more intensely will be apparent.

Intercourse and Ejaculation Mastery

After a few weeks of practice, when you have intercourse with your partner, you will, in effect, have to start the process over. The temptation will be to go into old patterns and ejaculate rather quickly. Take all the breaks you need and make sure your partner is helping you recognize your energy patterns. Loving partners play an important role in learning these techniques so enlist their help whenever you can.

This time the results should happen much sooner. Your body and mind will be working together so that you can consciously create the experience you want to have. Some men will take a little longer in this stage than others, but if you keep your conviction to have as much pleasure as possible and to give that to your partner too, you'll be fine.

Ultimately, you may be able to last for as long as you like. This will allow you to move into the realms of mystical sexual experience, should you choose to go there. You and your lover will be able to travel together to new heights of ecstasy.

FACT

It's reported that up to 75 percent of all men ejaculate within two to five minutes of beginning intercourse. A survey of 1,370 men conducted by tantra.com revealed that fewer than 35 percent felt they had any control over when they ejaculate.

Simultaneous Orgasms

Simultaneous orgasms sometimes happen to couples that spend a long time making love and are very attentive to each other. Having an orgasm at the same time as your partner is an ideal that is hard to count on achieving. The longer the man lasts and the more tuned in the woman is to her orgasmic response level, the more possible this elusive act is.

The deep knowing that occurs in long-time partnerships and with lovers who are very attuned to their partner's rhythms can help lead to the possibility of mutual orgasms. Staying aware of your lover's breath patterns, response levels, subtle movements, and reflexes will keep you in sync with each other's timing. The man who can last the time it takes for his lover to reach orgasm can begin anticipating her responses and then allow himself to reach the same climactic regions with her. This takes training and time to be able to count on it, some of the time. It is never a sure thing, but two people committed to training their response levels to parallel the other's can achieve this level of intimacy.

Achieving mastery at simultaneous orgasms is the beginning of the place that the master's called "Performing Sexual Magic." This art begins the world of the possibilities of union that borders on prayer. It is considered "High Sex" and is the ultimate jumping-off point for Tantric sex and a union so divine that the lovers become lost or blended as if they are but one being or energy.

Chapter 16

The Art of Relationship

The Kama Sutra has a generous amount to say when it comes to relationships between men and women. While a lot of it is for men about the kinds of women they should choose to associate with, it has also something to say about what women want in both their choice of partners and their needs as sensual beings. It goes on to say that the most important relationship is one of love, mutual respect, and harmonious partnership.

Selecting a Spouse

The Kama Sutra refers to ways of selecting and obtaining a spouse. Though ethically it was not the norm to marry for love, it was thought to be the best marriage possible.

"In order to bring about a marriage with a girl such as is desired, the parents and relations of the man should exert themselves, as should such friends on both sides as may be desired to assist in the matter. These friends should bring to the notice of the girl's parents, the faults, both present and future, of all the other men that may wish to marry her, and should at the same time extol even to exaggeration all the excellences, ancestral and paternal, of their friend, so as to endear him to them, and particularly those that may be liked by the girl's mother." —Part 3, Chapter 1, Sutras 4–6

The family of the girl would dress her and make sure that she was seen at community gatherings and holy festivals. They would seek out advise from astrologers and sages and put specific emphasis on certain young men. Very often a family would have a connection to another family and know of a young woman or young man whom they were interested in already. Sometimes—though rarely—a young woman and man would find each other, have an attraction, and invoke their parents and friends to help facilitate the marriage permission. "Marriage can bring many joys and sorrows. Because it is based on love, the gandharva marriage is the best" (Part 3, Chapter 5, Sutra 30).

FACT

The Kama Sutra cautions men not to seek out the wives of other men: "Who in his right mind lets drop what he holds in his hand in order to catch a dubious object?" And: "A pigeon to eat is worth more than a peacock in the sky."

Wooing the Young Woman

The Kama Sutra goes extensively into ways to connive, convince, set up, and manipulate men, women, parents, friends, servants, and any other helper one might select to help secure a marriage partner. "The suitor should always be on very cordial terms with the woman whom he thinks to be the girl's confidant, and as their acquaintance grows, he should consolidate their friendship" (Part 3, Chapter 3, Sutra 8). Bringing gifts, learning about things that the girl is interested in so that he might show knowledge in those same things, and contriving with the girl's nurse's daughter to arrange a meeting in private are all things suggested for the lovelorn young man.

◀ Wooing the young woman

Wooing the Young Man

Some of these same things might be done on the part of the girl, too. In addition she might sit next to him at a public gathering or wedding. She would increasingly make subtle advances like putting her foot on his or turning and causing her breast to brush his arm. They might secretively hold hands and play clever games together to show skill and charm. She might even be bold enough to arrange a private meeting somewhere. She would use a friend or trusted servant as a go-between.

Qualities and Duties of the Wife

Many of the qualities and duties of the wife are contained in the list of the Sixty-Four Arts. A good marriage brings many good fortunes to both families, though in Hindu society, the young woman goes to live in the young man's family compound. She was expected to cook, raise children, help with her elderly parents-in-law, show respect, and much more. A wife needed to be somewhat pious, perform religious duties, and be clever and resourceful.

"When a girl of the same caste, and a virgin, is married in accordance with the precepts of the Holy Writ (Dharma Shastras), the results of such a union are: the acquisition of Dharma and Artha, offspring, affinity, increase of friends, and un-tarnished love. For this reason a man should fix his affections upon a girl of good family, whose parents are alive, and who is three years or more younger than himself. She should be born of a highly respectable family, possessed of wealth, well connected, and with many relations and friends. She should also be beautiful, of a good disposition, with lucky marks on her body, and with good hair, nails, teeth, ears, eyes, and breasts, neither more nor less than they ought to be, and no one of them entirely wanting, and not troubled with a sickly body. The man should, of course, also possess these qualities himself." —Part 3, Chapter 1, Sutras 1, 2

Qualities and Duties of the Husband

A young woman will be attracted to a young man of courage and strength. He should be kind but firm, affectionate but not overly dependant, wealthy but not arrogant about it. He should have a good sense of self and feel independent of his mother and parents, in general. If he follows the precepts that life dictates including the knowledge of the arts of love, he will succeed in pleasing his wife and pleasing the gods. The man should also make a home for his wife.

"Having thus acquired learning, a man, with the wealth that he may have gained by gift, conquest, purchase, deposit, or inheritance from his ancestors, should become a householder, and pass the life of a citizen. He should take a house in a city, or large village, or in the vicinity of good men, or in a place, which is the resort of many persons. This abode should be situated near some water, and divided into different compartments for different purposes. It should be surrounded by a garden, and also contain two rooms, an outer and an inner one. The inner room should be occupied by the females, while the outer room, balmy with rich perfumes, should contain a bed, soft, agreeable to the sight, covered with a clean white cloth, low in the middle part, having garlands and bunches of flowers upon it, and a canopy above it, and two pillows, one at the top, another at the bottom. There should be also a sort of couch besides, and at the head of this a sort of stool, on which should be placed the fragrant ointments for the night, as well as flowers, other fragrant substances, things used for perfuming the mouth, and the bark of the common citron tree. Near the couch, on the ground, there should be a pot for spitting, a box containing ornaments, and also a lute hanging from a peg made of the tooth of an elephant, a board for drawing, a pot containing perfume, some books, and some garlands of the yellow amaranth flowers. Not far from the couch, and on the ground, there should be a round seat, a toy cart, and a board for playing with dice; outside the outer room there should be cages of birds, and a separate place for spinning, carving, and such like diversions. In the garden there should be a whirling swing and a common swing, as also a bower of creepers covered with flowers, in which a raised parterre should be made for sitting." —Part 1, Chapter 4, Sutras 1–15

Daily Activities

The Indian Hindus, now and in the ancient past, have always combined cleanliness, religious ritual, daily routine, and beauty into their existence. It is simply the way life is conducted, especially in the higher castes. Remembering that the Kama Sutra is a part of a triad—the Kama Sutras, the Dharma Sutra, and the Artha Sutras—you can see that one thing is tied to another. The activities of life are intricately linked to one another. All are performed with consciousness and attention to detail.

"Now the householder, having got up in the morning and performed his necessary duties (religious), should wash his teeth, apply a limited quantity of ointments and perfumes to his body, put some ornaments on his person and makeup on his eyelids and below his eyes, color his lips with alacktaka, and look at himself in the glass. Having then eaten betel leaves, with other things that give fragrance to the mouth, he should perform his usual business. He should bathe daily, anoint his body with oil every other day, apply a lathering substance to his body every three days, get his head (including face) shaved every four days and the other parts of his body every five or ten days. All these things should be done without fail, and the sweat of the armpits should also be removed. Meals should be taken in the forenoon, in the afternoon, and again at night. After breakfast, parrots and other birds should be taught to speak, and the fighting of cocks, quails, and rams should follow. A limited time should be devoted to diversions with learning, reading, and witticisms and then should be taken the midday sleep. After this the householder, having put on his clothes and ornaments, should, during the afternoon, converse with his friends. In the evening there should be singing, and after that the householder, along with his friend, should await in his room, previously decorated and perfumed, the arrival of the woman that may be attached to him, or he may send a female messenger for her, or go for her himself. After her arrival at his house, he and his friend should welcome her, and entertain her with a loving and agreeable conversation. Thus end the duties of the day." Part 1, Chapter 4, Sutras 16–25

▲ Daily worship practices

Women's Signs

The Ananga Ranga describes detailed psychological traits that a woman might display in various situations in her married life. These are rather fascinating and show a fine understanding of psychology of the woman. They detail her amorous signs, her signs of unhappiness, her signs of indifference, and the periods of her life that she will have the most desire for sexual connection. Most of these understandings are as true today as they were then.

Amorousness

An amorous woman will repeatedly fuss with her hair. She'll smooth it and fix it even though it may look just fine. She'll stroke her own cheeks, straighten her dress, and sometimes shift her clothing to make herself look more erotic. She'll chew or suck her bottom lip, sit a little off by herself, and sometimes a slight look of whimsy will cross her face.

She will embrace her female friend quite long, make jokes, and be sweetly loud and a little raucous. She'll stretch herself for no apparent reason, kiss children and boys, look at her own shoulders and limbs, and sob and sigh without apparent reason. She may yawn a lot and have a sleepy, sultry air about her. She does anything to distract her husband and gain his attention.

Coyness, drawing subtle attention to yourself, sort of showing yourself off, and being very bold and "in your power," so to speak, shows a self-worth that even the most demure and righteous woman can play at. Don't you know some women who are outrageous at this game and some who are wily and subtle?

Indifference

A woman may begin to show signs of indifference in her partnership or marriage. There are a variety of reasons for this, such as unspoken anger, mistreatment, worldly passion subsiding, dissatisfaction with a persistent action of her husband, or other things that she is not able to change or give advice about in the relationship. The acute awareness of these signs, on the part of ancient scholars, shows a culture that deeply studied and showed concern for these conditions.

Some of the signs of indifference are the feeling of unhappiness when her partner is happy, not looking her lover in the eye or responding when he speaks to her. She will be pleased when he leaves for a trip, she goes to sleep quickly, or avoids kisses and caresses by turning her head or her body away. She may go as far as to wish his friends and even his family ill-times, and she lacks appropriate respect for her husband's family.

Unhappiness

When a new bride's parents-in-law or new husband are stingy with word, deed, and worldly goods, it makes a bride unhappy. Being revered or having attention called to her when she is lighthearted and happy is difficult for a pious woman to handle. Women don't generally like to be held at an unreal level of esteem or awe by those they are very close to. They don't like to be constantly watched over or held to constrained levels of orderliness.

Work that is too hard, sickness, and being apart from their husbands too long are causes for unhappiness in women. Cruelty, abuse, bad language, and violence also play a part, as well as intimidation, threats, and suspicious thoughts about the woman's behavior. Poverty and too much sorrow are hard on women, especially if children are involved.

ALERT!

A husband who is unclean, dresses in a slack manner, or is impotent causes grief to women. If he has no regard for where or when they make love, and does not take the time to prepare sufficiently, the woman will not go willingly to lovemaking. If he shows no regard for her pleasure during sex, she will also consider herself very unfortunate.

Times of Greatest Desire

There are times in women's lives when they are most inclined toward sexual activities. Desire is the greatest and a woman is more easily satisfied at these specific times, too. The most general times are when their husbands or lovers have been gone a long time or, in the case of harem women, when they have not had a turn with the husband in a while.

The Ananga Ranga states that the easiest times to approach a woman for lovemaking are when she is tired from physical exercise and wants to lie down, when she is unusually merry, or when she is showing signs of shamelessness or is being bashful. Spring is the time of year most women become amorous. This can also occur in the early stages of pregnancy, one month after delivery, and right before and after her period. She will also feel amorous after a long fever or illness and especially during thunder, lightning, and rainy weather.

ESSENTIAL

As an exercise, have a heartfelt conversation about each of your experiences about sex. Be honest and vulnerable. Don't use blaming language; explain clearly, and then outline what you want. Each of you takes a turn and then each of you takes the time for a short wrap-up for anything you might have forgotten. Thank each other when you feel complete.

Relationships Today

Relationships were much easier in the time of the Kama Sutra. Marriages were generally arranged and society prescribed pretty rigid rules and cultural mores, which had to be followed. Life is very different today.

Many westernized people find themselves in new territory when it comes to relationships. New rules are being created daily by mass media, economic situations, church and state, political stances, laws, and a multitude of other influences. The rules shift and change constantly, and our hearts, heads, bodies, and souls have to follow best they can.

FACT

When partners can agree on the guidelines they would like to live by, many problems can be addressed quickly, and the relationship can grow to new heights. What they create together is the success—no matter what it looks like to the outside world. If it works for them, with deep communication, agreement, and trust, then that is a successful relationship.

Keys to Great Relationships

How you "do" sexual relations is a metaphor for your life. You can use your life or your sexual intimacy to make breakthroughs in your relationships. There are many things that have been said and can be said about good relationships. Here are some key items in the possible list, but there is much more that can be added.

Creating Intimacy

Doing "things" together does not equal intimacy. Having a deep, intimate connection during sex, and in your relationship, is about trusting yourself and your partner. When you give yourself over to vulnerable, open, playful sexuality, and a life philosophy that gently pushes your edges and keeps you taking gentle risks, you see how sweet and easy it is to deepen intimacy.

Taking Time

This is a big issue today with many people and relationships. You're so busy that you forget to have intimate fun. Try new Kama Sutra positions, talk to your lover, plan a get-away, or even a long evening for sensual interactions. The only solution is for you both to quit your jobs or, if you can't do that, schedule time.

The myth that sex has to be spontaneous is killing sex. Put it on your schedule and then, when the time comes, be spontaneous in the moment. Once in a while, though, schedule some time away, with no worries.

Trust and Presence

This is where trust comes in with a capital T. Trust comes from taking risks, and it paves the way for greater self-confidence and trust in life. Trusting relationships can be a wonderful foundation for deeper levels of risk-taking and self-knowledge.

Also, the exquisite gift of being 100 percent present with your lover will expand not only your level of intimacy, but will help build your skills as a lover, too. When you are present, you are more able to receive feedback and to learn.

Truth Telling and Being Responsible

Learning authentically loving ways to tell the truth will greatly improve all your relationships—both intimate and professional. Ask for what you want; don't do it if you don't want to; and don't fake anything.

You are responsible for your own pleasure, security, loving presence, and your own happiness. Your partner is not the responsible party. When you accept this responsibility fully for yourself and choose a partner who can do the same, your life together will be powerful.

Asking, Receiving, and Letting Go of Control

Teaching your lover how to treat you is a gift to both of you. It takes away the guesswork and opens the door for both of you to receive more loving. Some people are good receivers and some are better at giving. It is a rare and fortunate person who is good at both. Cultivating both qualities will give you greater pleasure in your relationship. Also, becoming sexually vulnerable and open may feel like the greatest of risks, but it yields huge benefits. Your safety depends on it—that is your sense of inner safety.

Life Involves Change

Our relationships will change over time. Some changes will be experienced as losses, others as gains. Each moment brings with it the possibility of something brand-new. Trying to hang on to what you have usually backfires. A good feeling cannot be held on to.

Similarly, an unpleasant feeling will often change to something else after it is expressed. Change cannot be controlled. It must be surfed—like the surfer who rides the wave, attempting to stay in the right relationship to the ever-changing movement of the water.

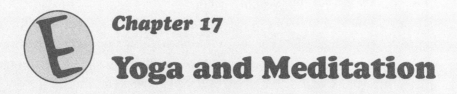

Chapter 17

Yoga and Meditation

The implications for upping the ante on your sexual response levels are enormous. The combinations of breath, focus, and increased consciousness work to bring more connection and orgasmic capacity to your relationship with yourself and your beloved. Yoga and meditation combine these aspects and keep you ready and able to try some of the more elaborate positions of the Kama Sutra!

Yoga

Practicing yoga, either alone or as a couple, will increase your flexibility. It will also increase your focus, which will aid in lovemaking. If you are partnered, the sexercises can be fun for not only movement but to play with gender equality and balance. These postures were chosen for their direct ability to promote sexual health.

Yoga is also another term associated with practices that help to unify apparent opposites. The practice of hatha yoga, for example, tones not only the muscles, it massages and keeps healthy the vital internal organs in our bodies as well. It harmonizes the body and the mind by connecting conscious breathing with focusing the mind.

When doing yoga, you are actually performing an active meditation. You are focusing your energy on certain internal, as well as external, points. You bring much more awareness to the body and mind with yoga.

Westerners see yoga as exercises to keep limber, but yoga is much more than that. Yoga focuses the mind, promotes health in the internal organs, and opens the practitioner to awareness of inner struggle and personal growth opportunities.

Solo Yoga Exercises

Solo sexercises can be done by yourself, or next to your partner. Choose a comfortable place in your home with a carpet. Use a yoga mat or an extra rug for more padding. Some soft music, much as you might use for a massage, may be appropriate.

The Cat

With your knees and hands on the floor, slightly hump your back and look down. Now look up and arch your back. When you look up, your back will arch naturally. Slowly and consciously go from one position to the other. Exaggerate the movement. Feel the release in your back. This keeps your hips limber and your lower back in great shape. It's excellent for pregnant women, too. Add an advanced move to this by squeezing your PC (pubococcygeus) muscles on the *in* breath and relaxing the pelvic floor completely on the *out* breath.

▲ The Cat Posture

The Butterfly

Sit on the floor and drop your legs to the side. Put the bottom of your feet together and pull your legs up slightly toward your crotch. They will be bent at the knees. Stretch like this, relax, stretch again, relax, and take a few deep breaths between stretches. However, try not to bounce; it's a subtle pressing on the knees. You can do this one before you get out of bed in the morning, too.

◀ The Butterfly Posture

The Squat and Stretch

Begin by squatting on the floor with your heels down and feet and legs spread comfortably apart. Put your hands under each of your feet with your fingers facing back. Gently push your forearms against your legs to give a stretch to the inner thighs. Now from this position, stand up and hang from the waist. Just let your head hang. Go back to the squat and stretch again.

◀ The Squat Posture

Chopping

Move into the squatting position with the hands down between your legs and hands folded, arms straight out in front. Now move the hands rapidly up, over the head, and bring them down again, in a chopping motion. Repeat.

FACT

Recent studies on oxytocin, a compound released during childbirth, breastfeeding, and sexual climax, show that it slows breathing, lowers blood pressure dramatically, and boosts the immune system. Along with orgasm, yoga and meditation do these same actions.

The Hug

Lie on your back and bring your knees up to your chest. Hug your legs tightly, then release a little and hug again. A variation is to cross your feet at the ankles and hug and then cross the other way and hug. You can also roll from right to left and forward and backward.

▲ The Hug Posture

Partnered Yoga Exercises

Partnered stretches, positions, and movements give couples a chance to be together in intimate ways without being sexual in that moment. You can increase your awareness of each other as well as your focus on the other's needs. Couples can help each other to improve in health, intimacy, vitality, and mobility when they work and play together at these sexercises.

Push-Me, Pull-You

Sit across from each other and spread your legs open. Touch feet and hold hands. Get comfortable. If one of you is much taller than the other one, adjust yourselves appropriately. Start out easily on this one. One of you leans back while the other leans forward. Hold the move and then reverse it.

If the man is a lot stronger or taller than the woman, he should let her lead the stretch so that she isn't overpowered. Continue leaning back and forth for the stretch. Try rotating around at the hips, being playful and creative with this exercise, too.

ALERT!

Stay aware of your partner and his or her needs. Don't overdo any stretch, especially if you are stretching someone else.

Heart Opener

Sit on the floor with your backs to each other. Sit up straight with your backs touching. Lock elbows and have one partner gently bend forward. Hold for a moment. Allow the person arching to get a good stretch. Think about opening up the heart area of the chest. Rise up and bend the other direction. The partner bending forward can remind the partner arching to focus on her heart. Do a few of these and do them slowly.

Standing Heart Opener

The exercise can also be done standing. This one is a great way to stretch the back and even free the joints of the spine. Let the person bending actually lift the person arching a few inches off the ground.

The Arch

One of the partners lies on the floor with knees bent and feet on the floor. His arms are down at the sides with the palms facing down. As this partner lifts his pelvis in an arch toward the ceiling, the standing partner helps him by gently aiding in the lift. The standing partner can be positioned over him with one foot on either side. This partner should bend and lift with the knees to prevent lower back strain.

FACT

Yoga is one of the fastest growing trends in America and celebrities have helped with that growth. *Yoga Journal* magazine estimates that 7 percent of the American population practices yoga today.

Nonsexual Yab/Yum

The man sits on the floor with his legs crossed and the woman sits on his lap, like in the sexual position Yab/Yum. She is facing him and has her legs wrapped around his body. Gently embrace and breathe slowly together. Try breathing together and then try breathing alternately. The woman should lead the breath pace, as women tend to breathe a little slower than men.

Mellow Contact Improvisation

Lie on the floor together and eye gaze for just a moment. Begin to move slowly toward each other by extending a leg, an arm, or another body part. The point is to move in unison around each other, while rolling and tumbling, and have your bodies stay in maximum contact while you move. This can be a wonderful exercise for couples to develop their connection and be in sync. You'll get smoother at it every time you try it. Sensuous music will help you to keep the flow of movement.

These exercises will allow both of you to become much more in tune with each other. A wonderful addition to these is to include a set of PC muscle sexercises, or Kegels, to the routine. Be inventive and add some new stretches to your repertoire.

Communicate with your partner during all of these sessions. Make sure that you both have each other's comfort zones in mind. There is plenty of time to improve on the stretch and become more limber. Take it easy the first few times.

Meditation

Meditation is being recognized, in many different circles today, for its value in bringing focus and quiet to the mind. Its simple techniques are easy to learn and are useful in a variety of ways in our lives. As little as twenty minutes a day can bring relaxation, concentration, and lower blood pressure to most people.

Focused Attention for Loving

Practicing meditation will enable you to focus your attention during lovemaking. Most people, at some time or another during sex, have found their mind wandering, or have found that they think about whether they are doing it right or about what they wish their partner would do. When you are more in the moment and less in the mind, your intuition takes over. Your lovemaking will get more creative and inspired.

The highest honor and gift you can give a partner is focused attention. When you bring that quality to your loving, it doesn't matter what techniques you know—you simply are a great lover.

Create a Meditative Space

You may want to consider creating an altar or area in your home that reflects the kind of energy you'd like to cultivate in your life. This can be a place where you put a goddess statue, symbolic items that have deep meaning for you, candles, incense, plants, and other sacred objects. Small books with daily gratitude sayings, seasonal additions, and pictures of loved ones can be added too.

If you are going to use this space for meditating, you'll want to consider a small cushion to sit on or a comfortable straight-back chair. A room that is far away from the hustle and bustle of your home is best. Add a small CD player if you're going to be doing yoga in this space, too.

FACT

In a recent study comparing relaxation techniques and meditation, scientists have discovered that meditation goes a lot farther in altering brain waves into a deeply relaxed state. In neural mapping of the brain, this state of mind looked similar to states of ecstasy when the participants focused on compassion for others.

Simple Meditation Techniques

Make yourself comfortable in your seat. If you are sitting on the floor on a cushion, sit cross-legged in the Lotus or Modified Lotus. If you place the cushion under your tailbone, you'll be able to sit longer in this position.

◀ The Half Lotus Meditation Pose

Close your eyes and begin soft belly breathing. Allow your thoughts to just float in and out of your consciousness without doing anything about them. Just watch them come and go. Focus on your *in* breath and your *out* breath. When your attention wavers to a thought, go back to the breath and focus your attention there again. Continue in this manner, always coming back to the breath.

Another technique for meditation is to focus on an object like a lit candle, a yantra, or even a single point in a picture. Place the object at eye level about two or three feet from your eyes. Your eyes should be open but just slightly. If your eyes get tired, close them and hold the vision of the image until it is lost. Open again and renew your gaze. Use the object as the focus point, much as the breath was in the other form of meditation.

Start with about fifteen minutes of sitting and work up to forty minutes a day. Be sure to move slowly when you are finished, perhaps even saying a prayer of gratitude before you rise to go on with your day.

The Chakras

In Eastern medicine, the chakras are seven "energy centers" situated along the spine in what is called the subtle body. Practitioners of Eastern medicine treat the subtle body as well as the gross physical body and see the chakras as very important to the overall health of the individual. The chakras are associated with the basic core energies that we work with in life.

◀ The positions of the seven Chakras in the body

Ayurvedic medicine, and other sciences studied during the era of the original Kama Sutra, related to the body, the mind, and the soul. Treatment for almost every ailment combined practice that covered all of these areas. Yoga was, and is today, studied not only for its importance to our flexibility and inward focus, but for the purpose of aligning the spine, the chakras, and for the active massage it gives our internal organs.

Here is a brief description of the seven chakras:

- **The First Chakra (Muladhara):** The first chakra is located at the base of the spine at the perineum, between the anus and the genitals. It represents being secure in the basic physical comforts of life: food, shelter, and the basics that keep us alive.
- **The Second Chakra (Svadhishthana):** The genital area is the seat of the second chakra. Our sexual urges, creativity, and procreation are the arenas of life that it represents. Sensations, pleasure, sexuality, and emotions are all associated with this chakra.
- **The Third Chakra (Manapura):** Willpower, energy, authority, self-esteem, and longevity are associated with the third chakra. It is situated at the solar plexus or navel area.
- **The Fourth Chakra (Anahata):** The chest area and specifically the heart are the home of the fourth chakra. It represents our heart and all that is associated with it—sharing, love, service, compassion, and devotion.
- **The Fifth Chakra (Vishuddha):** The fifth chakra represents knowledge and speaking the truth of that knowledge. It is situated in the throat area.
- **The Sixth Chakra (Ajna):** Located at the pineal gland or "third eye" area of forehead, the sixth chakra represents enlightenment and self-realization. Self-mastery, intuition, and insight are signs of an open sixth chakra.
- **The Seventh Chakra (Sahasrara):** This chakra is at the top of the head at the fontanel—the soft spot on a baby's head. It is the open conduit to God and the guru within.

Energy Meditations

Energy meditations involve conscious focus and some means by which to circulate the breath, the imagery, and the energy throughout the body and the mind. They might be best practiced, initially, by yourself and then with a partner. By learning and practicing any form of energy work, you will gain an advanced tool in the quest to ever more connection with the source of sensuous life within you.

Learning to relax and breathe more deeply is inherent to good sexual response. Faster breath can cause men to lose control over their ejaculation, but for women it will increase the pleasure and move her to orgasm sooner. When we breathe together, in the height of passion, we tend to match each other's speed, so use it wisely.

Breathing and Visualization

Begin by breathing into your belly—deep full breaths. Focus your attention on the *in* and *out* of the breath as you would during meditation. Feel your belly expand with the *in* breath and the air fall naturally from your body on the *out* breath. Practice this a few minutes.

When you feel comfortable with this way of breathing, sit on a straight-back chair or on the floor with a cushion just under the edge of your bottom. Sit Indian style with your legs crossed and begin to add a Kegel squeeze to the *in* breath and let it go on the *out* breath. Breathe *in* and *out* through your nose. Squeeze and relax with every breath.

You are creating a kind of energy "pump" when you breathe in and close the pelvic muscles to keep the energy in the body as you circulate it and then release it. Breathe slowly and get accustomed to this kind of breathing. Don't overdo the first few times.

The next step is to begin visualizing the breath going up your spine as far as the back of the inside of your skull and then out your nose. Imagine that the breath out is bathing your body with light. Breathe in again and imagine that the air is coming from the earth, up your spine, and out over the front of your body. It bathes you in radiant light and energy.

Now, you are ready to add a partner. Sit across from each other and practice this breath together. After a while, try alternating your breaths. You breathe in while your partner breathes out. This has the effect of both of you breathing in deeply the other's pheromones. Those are the odorless sexual attractants that draw us to one another. They get you turned on!

Add to your practice a faster breath. Do this for no more than ten breaths the first time. Pace yourselves. You will find this useful later during lovemaking when you want to increase the sexual charge and turn-on but also want to control the energy flow and his ejaculation rate.

Visualize orgasmic pleasure and it will follow. Move the energy being created in the body with the mind. Spread it throughout the body from the genitals. Circulate it. This will be a great key to a man's ability to master his ejaculation.

▲ Circulating energy between partners

Lovemaking

As you take this into your lovemaking, be patient with yourselves—it will come and you will reap the benefits of having practiced these meditations. Start your lovemaking in the Yab/Yum Position first. The man sits upright and the woman straddles him. He crosses his legs under her and she crosses hers behind his back. This is the close version of the earlier exercise. It allows you to undulate, breathe together, and eye gaze—all the makings of a grand energy meditation on love! Ⓔ

Chapter 18

E **Aphrodisiacs, Sex Aids, and the Occult**

Throughout history human beings have sought to enhance the sexual experience through eating, smoking, pleasure devices and toys, and through stimulation of the imagination. The Kama Sutra combined Ayurvedic principles, folk medicines, artificial phalli, and even piercing to create a treasure chest of erotic possibilities. As you will see from the compilation of sex aids in this chapter, almost anything can add to your pleasure if your mind associates it with sex.

What Is an Aphrodisiac?

An aphrodisiac is typically considered to be any substance that you either ingest or take part in to enhance pleasure. The list of possible aphrodisiacs is probably endless, since every person has had different early life experiences associating certain foods, odors, or environments with sex. For one person, whose mother used to give him chocolate milk while bathing him, chocolate milk might later be an aphrodisiac. For another, it could be the sound of the toilet flushing—since he used to flush the toilet when he masturbated in the bathroom!

Some of the well-publicized aphrodisiacs in ancient times were rhinoceros horn, elk antler, and powdered sea horse. Asiatic people have used these substances for thousands of years to produce heightened sexual response. There is little evidence that these substances actually work, however, and serious damage is being done to the environment today because of these ancient beliefs.

Things that mimic the shape of the phallus or the vulva have always been considered aphrodisiacs. Cucumbers, eggplants, orchids, bananas, and oysters all have a reputation. Spanish fly, soma from the ancient Asiatic cultures, and many plants including the datura plant have long had reputations for their erotic powers.

▲ The datura plant

Also, a good deal of evidence exists associating some everyday items with enhanced sexual interest or arousal. These things include erotic art, certain genital-like flowers, a sensual setting, watching a sexual video, reading erotic literature, compassion, vulnerability, looking at erotic books, deep breathing and relaxation, talking about sex, shared physical exercise, teasing and touch, words of love, certain smells and foods, and many herbs and extracts.

What other things turn you on?
Make a short list of items that increase your desire and stimulate your libido. Share this list with your lover and ask him or her to do the same. Notice the things that are the same and the ones that are different.

QUESTION?

Love Potions from the Kama Sutra

Love potions and aphrodisiacs have existed since the beginning of human consciousness. Desire and its conquest seem to be innate properties of human beings. In an established culture such as India's, the centuries of experimentation have given a few very juicy recipes for increasing potency and stamina, drawing a desired lover to you, and increasing arousal and sexual desire.

To Enslave a Lover

These recipes are folk remedies that were used in ancient times to enslave a lover who was not going along with your advances. More subtle recipes are used today. Wouldn't you rather drink a little champagne and eat oysters than dust your penis with powdered peacock bone? These things may work, though. What do you think?

- "Leaves caught as they fall from trees and powdered with peacock-bone and fragments of a corpse's winding-sheet will, when dusted lightly on the penis, bewitch any woman living" (Part 7, Chapter 1, Sutra 26).

- "If you crush milky chunks of cactus with sulphur and realgar, dry the mixture seven times, powder it, add honey, and apply it to your penis, you'll satisfy the most demanding lover" (Part 7, Chapter 1, Sutra 28).
- "And if, to these powerful ingredients, you add monkey's dung, grind them together and sprinkle the powder on your unsuspecting lover's head, she will be your devoted slave for life" (Part 7, Chapter 1, Sutra 30).

To Increase Potency

Today you might want to consider some of the more conventional methods of increasing potency and well-being, including healthy living, vitamins, and supplements. Even Viagra and the new pharmaceuticals that are coming to the marketplace might be a better source than sparrow eggs or monkey dung!

- "If ghee (clarified butter), honey, sugar, and licorice in equal quantities, the juice of the fennel plant, and milk are mixed together, this nectar-like composition is said to be holy, and provocative of sexual vigor, a preserver of life, and sweet to the taste"(Part 7, Chapter 1, Sutra 45).
- "Anoint your penis, before lovemaking, with honey into which you have powdered black pepper, long pepper and datura—you will completely satisfy your woman" (Part 7, Chapter 1, Sutra 25).
- "Honey-sweetened milk in which the testicles of a ram or a goat have been simmered has the effect, when drunk, of making a man as powerful as a bull" (Part 7, Chapter 1, Sutra 37).
- "Pumpkin seeds ground with almonds and sugarcane root, or with cowhage root and strips of bamboo, and stirred into honeyed milk, have the same arousing effect" (Part 7, Chapter 1, Sutra 39).
- "The sages say that wheat-flour cakes baked with honey and sugar and sprinkled with the powdered seeds of pumpkin and cowhage give one strength for a thousand women" (Part 7, Chapter 1, Sutra 42).
- "The yolk of a single sparrow's egg stirred into rice pudding that has been thickened with cream, wild-honey and 'ghee' has the same invigorating effect" (Part 7, Chapter 1, Sutra 43).

To Boost the Potential of the Penis

The use of wasps and other stinging insects to increase the girth and length of the lingam was well known in ancient India. But today, this seems a wild and risky technique. Undoubtedly this practice was done under the direction of a qualified physician, or Ayurvedic practitioner.

- "Take shuka hairs—the shuka is an insect that lives in trees—mix with oil and rub on the penis for ten nights, take it off then put it on again. When a swelling appears sleep face downwards on a wooden bed, letting one's sex hang through a hole" (Part 7, Chapter 2, Sutra 25).
- "Thus having obtained the desired result, get rid of the pain with a cooling mixture made of five astringents. This is the way to eliminate the pain caused by the swelling. The swelling caused by a shuka lasts for life" (Part 7, Chapter 2, Sutra 26).
- "By rubbing it successively with the juice of ashvagandha, or shabara roots, or jala shuka, or brihati, or buffalo butter, or hastikarna, or vajracalli the penis will stay swollen for one month" (Part 7, Chapter 2, Sutra 28).
- "A man who climaxes too swiftly should arouse his lady by caressing her clitoris with his fingers and flooding the well of her yoni before he enters her" (Part 7, Chapter 2, Sutra 2).
- "If, during lovemaking, the erection cannot be sustained because the man is old, or simply exhausted he should use the delicate oral techniques given in an earlier chapter" (Part 7, Chapter 2, Sutra 3).

The Kama Sutra also goes into great detail about additions the man can have inserted into the foreskin of his lingam. A young man would first perforate his lingam and then stand in water until the bleeding stopped. He should then make love several times a day for several days so the wound won't heal. He should wash it with various ointments to keep it clean for several weeks. He then proceeds to widen the hole with objects designed for that use.

Many types of items are then used to insert into the hole. They could be tubular, triangular, knobby, pointed, or round. The lingam would then adjust over the years to larger and larger items.

FACT

Many cultures throughout history, and even today, use scarification as a sex aid. Typically, it will involve the man actually splitting portions of his lingam and then inserting objects into it to widen and lengthen his phallus. It can be likened to ear and body-part piercing.

Sex Aids

Sex aids were also known in the ancient India, and were employed for certain reasons. Though it doesn't appear that they were used on a regular basis, they were crafted so that a husband and wife could continue amorous intimacy even if the man was not able to manage it on his own. They appear to be made of quite interesting materials and were best designed to match the lingam of the person that they replaced. To increase the size or proportions of his lingam, a man also wore artificial phalluses over his own.

"The man who is utterly unable to achieve an erection should pleasure his wife/lover with a phallus crafted from materials like gold, silver, copper, iron, ivory or horn. The artificial phallus should be shaped to your natural proportions. It will be more arousing for the lady if the outside is studded with a profusion of large, smooth nodules" (Part 7, Chapter 1, Sutras 4–8).

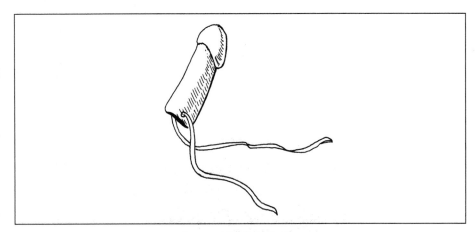

▲ An artificial phallus

Vatsyayana's Cautions

Throughout the text of the Kama Sutra, Vatsyayana encourages caution and regard for both the man's and the woman's preferences. He shows a true voice of sanity when he concludes that, after all of the instruction and the many aphorisms, the couple should always choose for themselves the ideas and practices that suit them best. He encourages citizens to use professionals and to proceed with caution in experimentation of all sorts.

- "A person who wishes to avail of such recipes in the conduct of his love affairs should study them from the Ayurveda and the Tantric texts or otherwise from persons who are acquainted with the practices" (Part 7, Chapter 1, Sutra 49).
- "Recipes about which the user has the slightest doubt or which cause physical harm, or the killing of some living animal, or which recommend the use of impure ingredients, must be avoided" (Part 7, Chapter 1, Sutra 50).
- "Only those practices found effective after long trial, approved of by cultured people and blessed by Brahmins and friends, should be resorted to" (Part 7, Chapter 1, Sutra 51).
- "The ways and means which have been enumerated earlier for the purpose of increasing a man's passion are to be practiced only by those who are absolutely in need of them. They are emphatically forbidden to those who do not need to use them" (Part 7, Chapter 2, Sutra 54).
- "It is not to be understood that simply because this work mentions certain artifices and expedients, that they are to be used by all and sundry. While the Science is certainly meant to be studied by everybody, the practice of these expedients should be restricted to particular persons who need them" (Part 7, Chapter 2, Sutra 55).

Chemicals of Love

Pheromones are subtle odor-producing substances given off by our bodies. We respond physiologically to another person's "scent," even if we cannot consciously smell it. The word *pheromone* is derived from a Greek word meaning "to transfer excitement." Body temperature, skin conductance, heart rate, and blood pressure are just some of the functions that can be affected by our reactions to other people's pheromones.

Pheromones don't have a smell or odor that is discernable, but humans have special detectors in their noses for pheromones. They can be covered up by colognes and perfumes, which mask the effect they have. So before you put on your favorite cologne, consider what you may be giving up.

Research on Pheromones

British researchers have discovered that pheromones affect our attraction to the opposite sex. During a controlled study, women were asked to rate men's pictures according to body shape, face appeal, and other characteristics. During part of the study, the researchers dabbed the rooms with male pheromones. The pictures that the women were asked to evaluate, all of a sudden, got better ratings, especially the previously "average" men. This was particularly true for women in the midpoint of their monthly cycles and the ones who did not take oral birth control. Women taking oral contraceptives seem to be less responsive to pheromones.

Other studies have shown that women who live together, over a period of time, or in close proximity, often have the same menstrual cycles. This occurs in households were there are at least several daughters and a mother, college dorms, and among women's sports teams. Pheromones seem to be the regulator causing this synchronizing effect.

Arousal Aids

Some men and women are greatly attracted to the smell of their partner's underarms and hair. Male and female pheromones are excreted from glands in the hair follicles, the underarms, and the groin area. Try burying your nose in your partner's hair the next time you want to become aroused.

It's said that there is an old custom for men to bury their handkerchiefs under their arms while dancing and then to present the handkerchief to their partner at the end of the dance. Maybe the relatively new advances, like deodorants and scented soaps, have been detrimental to lovers!

FACT

Pheromones are available for purchase and can be added to your favorite perfume or dabbed on separately. The jury is out on their effectiveness since there haven't been many studies done with manufactured pheromones. They aren't too expensive, so try some out for yourself.

Scents and Perfumes

Scents and perfumes have been used since time immemorial, possibly to mimic pheromone's actions. One of the most popular is musk, which has a smell very close to the male hormone testosterone. The Romans used civet and ambergris as the carriers for lavish perfumes that were erotic in nature.

Vanilla, lavender, and flower essences have been used for thousands of years to add allure to our already present bodily scents. Also, many of the tropical forests in Hawaii were cut down in the eighteenth and nineteenth centuries for the delicate scent of sandalwood. Its wood carries the musky, earthy scent that the finest European fans, for aristocratic women, were made from. This wood never loses its scent, so it served as a perfume when a woman seductively fanned herself.

Picking a Perfume

When choosing a perfume, if you like wearing one, pick something that isn't too overbearing. It should complement the subtle scent of your own skin, hair, and pheromones. Try going without perfume sometimes, especially before a night of lovemaking. This goes for men, too. Don't always wear colognes. They can distract from wonderful, naturally erotic smells.

Massage and Essential Oils

Some fun additions to a sex-positive bedroom are wet, slippery massage oils. They will help you have a better time when you make love. They're fun to put on your own body and on your lover's body. They teach us to touch with grace and erotic goodwill.

Massage oils are fabulous for soothing massages as well as erotic massages. They should not go into the body, however. Keep them on the outside. Choose a scent that you think you and your lover would like. If it smells erotic, it's the right one for you.

ALERT!

Scents are best when they are natural, essential oils that are created to give the ultimate sensual experience. Popular essential oils used for erotic purposes are vanilla, musk, orange, ylang-ylang, rose, cedarwood, geranium, lavender, and lemongrass. Look for blends that turn you on.

You may even want to try making your own—experimenting with different combinations of scents. If you decide to do this, you'll find the leftover essential oils you buy are a wonderful addition to the sensuous baths you and your lover will take. Simply add a few drops to the next bath for a heightened experience.

Incense

The use of incense has a long history for enhancing the setting in which lovemaking takes place. Again, pick something that is appropriate and not overbearing. You might want to place it in an adjacent room like a bathroom so that the hint of it reaches you rather than having the full strength take over the room you are in. You can also "freshen" a room with incense and then put it out quickly, to give just a hint of the scent.

Asian cultures still use incense to carry their prayers to the gods and goddesses they honor. Temples in China, Singapore, Indonesia, Malaysia, and India are everywhere and the sweet smoke of incense wafts to the streets freely. As the Asians associate it with prayer, you can associate incense with lovemaking. By lighting it and letting the smell gently spread through your house, you can signal a lover that you are thinking about sensual sex.

The Kama *Foodra*

It's often been said that food is the way to a man's heart. Well, that can have a lot of different implications. Healthful eating is of course the optimum for all of us. Certain foods do have a positive effect on the libido. Indian foods are generally highly spiced and contain spices that are beneficial to our circulatory system and our brain functions.

Oral Courses

If you are planning an evening of lovemaking that includes food, make eating a part of the ritual or ceremony of loving. That way, you can design eating into the sensual evening without it stopping the action. Eating can be a fun addition. You can feed each other. Eat in courses so that eating takes a lengthy time and is spread into courses between the "courses" of love.

Serving things like sushi, light pastas, small skewers of vegetables and fish, or a salad with many goodies in it would be perfect before lovemaking. The dessert could come later. Maybe you can present dessert on your inner thighs or offer your partner the opportunity to become the platter.

Suggestive Shapes

Many of the folk recipes for increased potency in the Kama Sutra involve foods that are elongated in shape. Try forming foods into shapes that are suggestive or downright sexual, like penises, breasts, and vulvas. These can be chocolates, little cakes, oysters, candies, breads, and main dishes. Your imagination can take you anywhere with this.

Soak dried fruit in wine or liquors to enhance its flavor. Use fresh and dried fruit to dip into sauces that are sweetened and have a yogurt base. Dip fresh fruit into chocolate or butterscotch sauces. Raspberry sauce, whipped cream, even ice cream in moderation, can be used in erotic ways to enhance an evening of love.

Spice Up Your Life

Some spices, seasonings, and foods with certain amino acids are good for raising the "heat." Adding a variety of spices to your food concoctions can have a wonderful effect of heightening arousal. Pumpkin pie spices, licorice, cinnamon, peppermint, curries, coriander, cardamom, lavender, chili peppers, sesame seeds, saffron, nutmeg, pepper, ginger, onions, and garlic are also considered aphrodisiacs by many cultures, and so are asparagus, figs, grapes, almonds, oysters, mussels, caviar, basil, bananas, and mangos.

QUESTION?

How do I find out what works for me?
Anything can be erotic, so create foods that appeal to you and your lover. It's fun creating and discovering new things together, and the time spent attending to the details will be rewarded. You are cocreating a ritual to honor your lovemaking.

Chocolate

One of the active ingredients in chocolate produces phenylethylamine, the chemical that the body manufactures when we fall in love. These chemical messengers speed up the flow of information that travels between our nerve endings. Phenylethylamine is similar in many ways to amphetamine, which dilates the blood vessels and creates energy and focus. It is not by chance that chocolate is so highly associated with love.

When the conquistadors invaded Mexico, Montezuma was reported to have drunk up to fifty cups a day of chocolate with chili and spices in it. He had to keep his stamina up to satisfy his many wives. Some women, as their hormonal balance shifts, crave chocolate as an unconscious remedy to lift spirits and provide energy.

Liquor

Used in small amounts, alcohol can enhance the sensual/sexual experience. It can relax you and ease your inhibitions. In small amounts, it has been cited as an aid in helping men last longer so they don't ejaculate too fast. In larger amounts, it has the opposite effect. "Consuming Dhattura fruit, or its diluted juice, causes intoxication" (Part 7, Chapter 2, Sutra 44).

Try using it in a ritual way by creating ceremony when you drink it. Sip it during lovemaking. Share a kiss, with a little liquor in your mouth. Let it dribble down your cheeks.

Take some liquor into your mouth and then give your partner oral sex while you still have it in your mouth. Throw in the element of surprise. This can add new sensations to both your experiences. It can be licked and sucked off if any gets away from you!

ALERT!

Amaranth flowers were considered particularly reflective of amorous intentions and were auspicious for lovers. Absinthe is a strong liqueur that is made from the amaranth plant. It has been made since the edge of time. It can be deadly in large doses, but it has aphrodisiac properties in small amounts.

The Occult and Astrology

Astrological compatibility was one of the destiny signs that the family considered important to the occasion of marriage. A bride's and groom's families, often before they had ever met each other, would have the charts compared for compatibility, birthing possibilities of the bride, and any potential areas of struggle that the young couple might encounter. Conception and the birth of babies were planned for certain days and periods of time, as well as any ceremony that had auspicious undertones. Magical rites were practiced and astrologers were a part of both kingly courts and village councils. Knowledge of these things was part of the Sixty-Four Arts one could learn.

- "Consulting the omens refers to the signs of destiny, omens deriving from the position of the planets, their conjunctions, influence, and meaning for the boy's future, foretelling a happy destiny for him" (Part 3, Chapter 1, Sutra 6).
- "Having consulted the omens, the date of the meeting is decided on, then that of the marriage ceremony" (Part 3, Chapter 1, Sutra 17).
- "The art of framing mystical diagrams, of addressing spells and charms, and binding amulets" (Part 7, Chapter 2, Sutra 48).
- "If, after smearing his palm with the excreta of the peacock who has partaken of Haritala and Manahshila, a person touches any object, he makes it invisible" (Part 7, Chapter 2, Sutra 46).
- "The eye of a peacock or a Tarakshu, covered in a golden amulet and worn on the right wrist or upper arm, is efficacious in beautifying oneself. The amulet must be sealed at an auspicious moment for this to work" (Part 7, Chapter 1, Sutra 10).

Clearly time, intent, and even place are to be taken into consideration in the pursuit of mystical activities. The use of secret language was common, especially in the pursuit of a lover. And the Yantras involved in the religious duties of the citizen's life required artistic abilities, as well as mystical formulas.

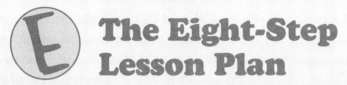

Chapter 19

The Eight-Step Lesson Plan

It is always helpful to have a plan and steps to follow that build to a deeper, more satisfying sexual experience. You will be able not only to get started with your new knowledge, but also to have a structure by which to grow and add your own creative ideas. The Eight-Step Lesson Plan, arranged in eight weeks, is accompanied by inquiry questions about the experience and about what might have been going on inside you and your partner.

Before Starting

Most of the eight-week lessons have been designed to practice solo or with a partner. Some of the practices require a partner but don't necessarily need to involve a sexual partner. You can enlist the partnership of a friend who may be interested in personal growth and upping the ante on his or her sex life, too.

The first four sets of practices should be continued throughout the entire lesson plan, as they are the foundation for the true transformation of your sexual experience. They are life enhancing and will outlast even the best sexual techniques and positions. The chapters that detail each of the lessons will be noted, when appropriate, so that you can brush up on the finer points if you need to.

Breathing

How we breathe is of the utmost importance to our vital health, both physically and emotionally. We need to retrain ourselves to breathe deeply and relax. Breathing, or rather lack of it, is one of the primary reasons women are preorgasmic or frustrated with their inability to orgasm every time. When men begin to notice their breath, slow it down, and relax in sexually exciting situations, they gain control over how long they can last during intercourse.

FACT

When you are new to breath exercises, you may hyperventilate in the beginning. You'll know because you'll get tingly and might feel dizzy. Slow down or even go back to your old way of breathing for a few minutes. Then, start again. You'll soon get beyond this.

If you are a woman, observe yourself the next time you are making love, either with your partner or by yourself. You feel good, you're at a level 9, the energy is building, your body gets tense and then tenser, suddenly, you notice that you're not breathing. What's happened?

This is a typical response pattern. You get tense and stop breathing. The orgasmic energy falls away and you have to build it again, often with the same results. The key is to learn to let the breath carry your sexual response.

If you are a man, observe yourself the next time you are self-pleasuring or making love with your partner. Do you notice that you are breathing hard and fast? What part of your body is your breath in? Can you slow down your breathing and deepen it while maintaining your erotic heights of pleasure?

The Practice

What we will work toward is a steady, full, deep breath into our bellies. This is a great practice for beginning meditation, also. It requires focus and attention plus relaxation. Allow about ten minutes for this practice. Every day would be ideal, either before you get up or just before you go to sleep.

Breathing through your nose is considered a "cool" breath, while breathing through your mouth is considered "hotter." In terms of the buildup of sexual energy, mouth breathing naturally happens when you are turned on and in the 8 to 10 zone of sexual excitement. You can also create "heat" by breathing through your mouth.

Lie on your back in a comfortable, quiet place. Don't use a pillow under your head. Close your eyes and place one of your hands on your belly. Begin a slow inhalation through the nostrils. Let your stomach rise with the breath and fall back on the *out* breath, almost in an exaggerated manner. Notice the rise and fall of the hand you've placed on your belly. Notice the slight arch in your back rising and falling with each breath.

After ten of these breaths, open your mouth slightly and on the exhalation let the air out slowly and softly through your pursed lips (a little sound is okay). Continue to breathe slowly and deeply in this manner. Notice the moment between the inhalation and the beginning of the exhalation. Expand that moment slightly. Relax and then relax even more deeply. Keep your mind on what you are doing.

Advanced Practice

Lie on the floor, again without a pillow under your head. Bring your knees up and place your feet on the floor, about hip-distance apart, just beyond your bottom. Relax your knees a little and let them hang out slightly or open up from your hips.

Begin to belly breathe and exaggerate the motions. As your belly fills with air, your back arches away from the floor and your hips rotate out to the front. Your chin will naturally move down, onto your chest. As you exhale, your head goes back and your spine flattens some to the floor. Your hips rotate back.

Do this move combined with the breath several times. Do you feel the body motion created by the breath movement? Your hips will be rotating back and forward as you breathe, and produce a kind of thrusting motion. They go forward on the *in* breath and backward on the *out* breath. Now try picking up the speed a little. Go easy at first and slowly pick up the speed. Continue the rocking and the breathing for a few minutes.

ALERT!

Only do what feels comfortable at any one moment. You can always come back to the exercise. Don't continue if you feel like you're off balance in any way. Everyone requires some adjustment time when making changes and learning new things. Be gentle with yourself and have fun.

This is a great lower-back relaxer, but it gives the motion of a dance to the thrusting, and really allows you to coordinate the movements of breath, hips, flow of the head and neck, and whole body into the breathing experience.

Inquiry

Ask yourself these five questions. By taking a point of reference about yourself now, you'll be able to notice how much you are expanding and growing later. Ask them separately for the main practice and then the advanced practice.

1. How did this make you feel?
2. Was it easy or a little uncomfortable at first?
3. Did you hyperventilate a little at first?
4. Did you have any judgments come up about expanding your belly?
5. Did you have any emotional reactions during this exercise?

The next time you self-pleasure or make love, observe your breathing patterns, if you can. If you have a partner, you may want to ask him or her to observe you. See what you notice. Breathing is covered in Chapter 5 if you would like to refresh your understanding before you try this exercise again.

Hand on Heart Eye Gazing

Eye gazing is a simple and profound practice. It requires being present and in the moment. Though eye gazing may look easy, it is not for some people. When eye gazing, there is nowhere to go and nothing to do. You just gaze into each other's eyes. There is no need to smile, frown, or give any eye and facial signals. In fact, don't do this. Just gaze at your partner and be fully present with him or her.

FACT

Learning to accept yourself and your lover without smiling, cracking jokes, or controlling them is liberating. Simply "being" with your partner and seeing into his or her soul through the eyes is a deepening, calming experience.

The Practice

Begin by sitting across from each other. You can be sitting cross-legged, on the bed or on chairs. Place your right hand on your partner's chest, between the breasts, and place your left hand over his or her hand on your chest, to hold it. If you are solo, do this with the mirror—it may even be a more profound way of doing this exercise.

Begin to breathe together. Softly look at each other. No need to stress or strain. Don't analyze the face across from you. Just gaze and breathe. If you giggle or squirm, as you might in the beginning, come back to the breath; it will focus you.

Spend ten minutes in this practice. After a few minutes, when you feel stable, observe which eye you have been looking into. Typically one or the other of your partner's eyes will be more comfortable to look into. See if you can notice this about yourself.

◀ Eye gazing and cycling the breath

Advanced Practice and Inquiry

An advanced step is to cycle the eyes in this exercise. As you breathe in, you each look into the left eye—as you breathe out, you each look into the right eye. When you've tried that, reverse the eyes. How does that feel? One direction of cycling may be more comfortable than another.

The Taoist's understanding of the balance in life, as exemplified by the yin/yang symbol, is that each individual has a feminine and a masculine side. When these are in balance, the individual is healthy and balanced, too. The left eye is the receptive, receiving, or yin eye, and the right eye is the active, giving, or yang eye. Noticing which of your eyes is more comfortable giving and which is more comfortable receiving is a data point for understanding your own balance.

Spend some time talking about this exercise with your partner.

1. How was it for each of you?
2. What made you squirm, if anything?
3. Could you sustain the ten minutes?
4. If you tried the advanced part, speculate on why one way of cycling might be more comfortable than the other. What did you discover?

Focusing Attention

One of the things that meditation teaches is focus—on the breath and on being in the moment. Life gives us ample opportunity, during the day and the night, to practice focus. Try each of these activities, along with your breath work, and "being conscious" will begin to occur for you more often.

Out in nature, stop what you are doing and just observe something close up. It can be a leaf, a branch, the effect the wind has on an object, cloud formations, water—anything. Contemplate what you are witnessing. Remember to breathe.

ALERT!

The next time you are making love, look deeply into your lover's eyes. Stay immersed in them and focused. Experience the whole event from that perspective, if possible. Keep your eyes wide open. Come back to your breath if your attention lapses.

Give close attention to how you are touching someone. Be very deliberate in the touch quality you offer. Put your attention on what you are doing. During touch and stroking, notice if your own fingers feel exquisite to you. Try meditating for ten to fifteen minutes. Follow your breath. It is okay to notice when you get uncomfortable or antsy. Just take note and come back to the breath.

The Goal and the Inquiry

The goal is to focus your attention more often. How did this go for you? Did you notice that it was difficult just to stop and observe something? How did the awareness at work go? Did you try meditating? When you begin to put attention on things that are unconscious for you, you see how present they are in your life. Keep practicing.

Kegel Sexercises

The PC muscle sexercises, known as Kegel sexercises, increase blood flow to the pelvic region, which aids in the increased flow of hormones and helps engorge the vaginal area. Those are also the sexercises that strengthen the pubococcygeal muscle—the muscle that starts and stops the flow of urine in both men and women.

As long as you do these exercises in a somewhat logical manner, you don't need to follow the exact order they are presented in. Modify your learning to best serve you and your lover.

It can't be stressed enough the benefits you will get from learning and doing these sexercises. First read about the proper way to learn to do these exercises in Chapter 8. Begin to practice them as often as you can remember. Put up little notes to yourself as reminders.

As you begin to get comfortable with your practice, notice any changes that might be occurring. You can do the "base line" test you might have done when you started to see if you notice a change. Don't be too discouraged if you don't notice much of a change. This takes a little time, as any muscle-conditioning exercise does.

Advanced Practice and Inquiry

Beyond the advanced practices in Chapter 8, try combining your breath with the Kegel practices. Sip fairly quick breaths in as you let your

PC muscles go and then contract them as you breathe out. You can do this through your mouth or through your nose.

You'll get better and better as you practice. Eventually, you will bring this combination to lovemaking. You'll be able to both breathe and pump your way to freeing your orgasm, or in the case of men, retain your ejaculate and expand your orgasm.

After finishing this exercise, ask yourself these four questions:

1. How do your muscles feel? After the first day? After a week? After a month?
2. Do you notice any "turn-on" when you do the exercises?
3. After about a month, can you begin to isolate the different muscle groups that comprise the pelvic floor?
4. If you are partnered, has that person noticed any change during intercourse?

Coming to Your Senses

Tantric philosophy says that the search for knowledge is in everything you do, see, and experience. That is why sensuality and sexuality are such important components of the Kama Sutra path. Being aware of your body, and all that it is capable of, teaches you exquisite lessons. That's why advanced civilizations, such as India's was, detailed the lessons of sexuality and the importance the senses bring to lovemaking.

ALERT!

The point of this exercise is to treat your partner to a complete sensory experience and to have fun. When you block one of the senses, the others become heightened. You can then experience them more deeply and become "aware" of their essences. You can come to, and rely on, your senses again.

Your senses of sight, touch, smell, taste, and sound aren't typically in your consciousness, yet they are the substances of life and you cannot be without them. The erotic feel of a soft breeze over your skin may not faze you any longer. You wolf down your dinner even though a gourmet chef delicately prepared it. Your lover's touch may not thrill you any longer, either. It is simply that you are not paying much attention.

The Practice

Create an evening with your lover that brings you back to your senses. Combine any of the following to create an adventure for both of you. If you aren't partnered now, you can still do this exercise with yourself by modifying some of the parts. Obviously, you won't be able to blindfold yourself. Treat it as a pleasure ritual.

Bathe each other and towel each other dry. Move slowly and with intention and focus. Decide who will go first; then blindfold the receiver and lay him or her down on your bed. Treat your lover to different modalities of touch: a feather, a rose, a makeup brush, a piece of fur, a piece of velvet, and see if she can identify what it is you are using. Blow on your partner softly. Trail a silk scarf or your hair over the length of his or her body.

◀ Creating a sensual experience

Pass bits of fruit under the nose of your lover for him to identify or just enjoy smelling. Try a flower from your garden. Dab a bit of perfume or an essential oil on your fingertips and wave it in the air. Use things that are subtle.

Gather a small bell, a chime, your charm bracelet, some dry leaves on a branch, a crystal glass to ring, a Tibetan bowl, or anything else you can think of that would produce exquisite sounds for your partner to experience. Even bending close to her ear and breathing softly will work.

You can have fun evaluating each of the new positions as you do them. This will also help you two fine-tune them to your particular body needs. You may also come up with new variations of your own.

Have your partner taste the different fruits you earlier passed by his nose now. A bit of whipped cream, chocolate, or liqueur would do nicely, too. Make small bits and use things that might not be expected.

Inquiry

After finishing this exercise, ask yourself these five questions:

1. How did you like being blindfolded? Was this "edgy" or difficult?
2. Did you surrender to the experience fully?
3. Did your partner introduce anything that you didn't like or you reacted to? If so, how did you respond?
4. Did you remember to breathe deeply? Did your partner remind you?
5. Did any of your senses seem to be heightened because you were blindfolded?

Man-Superior Positions

Set aside an evening to play and try out some new positions. Start with an hour or so of massage, foreplay, and oral sex, if you like it. You might even want her to have a clitoral orgasm first. Make sure you have some firm pillows that you can easily reach.

Throughout this encounter, stay very conscious and have a soft light on so you can see your partner. Remember and remind each other to deep breathe and relax. There is no need to rush anything. Just hang out in the fun and the juicy energy together. Men, if you need to take breaks between positions and you get a little soft, have your honey give you oral sex while you are on your knees in an upright position. This is a more yang position and you'll get harder, faster.

The Practice

When you are ready for intercourse, begin in the basic Missionary Position. From this position the woman should then bring her legs up over the man's hips so that she can leverage herself a little better. When you've tried this position, then move your legs and feet even higher on his body. Wrap them around him and lock your feet, if he isn't too big. Notice how well you can lift and move your hips.

Now put one leg over the shoulder of your partner. This isn't as hard as it seems. Here's where the pillows come in handy. Place one or two of them under buttocks so that the hips are lifted and cocked forward. The other leg can hang out in a wide-open position. Try adjusting this leg up and down, back a little and forward a little to see which subtle changes seem best for G-spot friction. Switch legs and try the same moves with the opposite side.

Now put both legs over your partner's shoulders. Try lifting your pelvis with your legs on his shoulders. This won't impact him. Men, you can put your hands under your partner's buttocks for support. This will also help you bring her closer when you are thrusting. Once you get into this position, you'll find movement easy and free for adjusting for just the right stimulation in just the right places.

FACT

More advanced positions derived from this one include the woman pressing her hands on the man's chest and pushing her legs and buttocks away from him. This puts penetration at an even more extreme angle. She can also put her feet on his chest, though this is fairly advanced.

Inquiry

Keep the following questions in mind when you are trying different positions. If you have set aside enough time for this practice, it won't interrupt the spontaneity if you are communicating about what you are learning and feeling.

1. Women, did you notice any difference with the angle that the lingam penetrated the yoni in each of the sets of positions? What seemed better for you—the higher your legs were or the lower they were?
2. Men, did you notice the angle? Were you more aroused when she had her legs lower or higher?
3. Did you have a difficult time controlling your ejaculation response in some of the positions, men? Was it hard for you to try this many positions and not ejaculate? Did you take breaks?
4. As a couple, did you find a couple of new positions that really got you excited?
5. Briefly interview each other and ask a few specific questions about anything connected with the different positions that might be concerning you.

Woman-Superior Positions

The secret Tantric sects that followed the practices of the Kama Sutra, and more esoteric practices too, believed that the woman was the goddess incarnate. She had the sensual power to lead the man in sexual activities that were heavenly. The woman-superior positions give modern women a chance to show that this principle was and is true.

Make sure you do this set of positions at a different time than the previous lesson. Men, having your woman on top may be very erotic, especially if it is the first time for you. Make sure you give yourself lots of breaks if you feel like you might ejaculate too soon. Take it easy!

As with your previous evening with the man-on-top positions, begin by engaging in a generous amount of foreplay. The more turned on the both of you are, especially the woman, the more fun you'll have trying these new positions. Warm her up well so that she feels turned on and empowered.

The Practice

When the two of you feel ready, start by having the woman lie on top of the man. Just lie there without having intercourse for a few minutes. Kiss and hug. While still lying down on his chest, wrap your legs around your partner, women, and help him to insert his lingam into you. Bring your knees up a little to rest on the bed and place your feet flat to help you create traction.

ALERT!

Stay in communication with your partner at all times when you're both learning. If you don't give feedback, you won't feel empowered enough to lead in the creative areas, either. You'll both expand and grow faster if you do.

Begin to rock up and down a little, rubbing your body on his and focusing on your clitoris, in the direction from your head to your feet. Now lift up a little and bring your hips up and down on his lingam. Try experimenting with deep thrusts and more shallow thrusts in this position.

Now sit up on top of him. Keep your knees on the bed with your feet flat or relaxed. Thrust by moving up and down. Churn your hips in small circles and from side to side. You can use thrusting patterns from Chapter 8 to help you get creative.

This is an excellent position to employ thrusting techniques in. You can act as "the Bumble Bee" by staying high and shallow on the head of his lingam or plunge deeper every second or third time. Choose your rhythm and speed carefully. You are in charge—you don't want him to go over the top too quickly.

Inquiry

Ask yourself these questions after completing this practice:

1. Did you find yourselves inventing other variations on these positions? Did you try turning around on him to face his feet?

2. If this was your first time on top, was it difficult for you or did you feel secure and loved?

3. Did you find yourself worrying or wondering how you looked? Did you let go of it? If you did, what happened to allow you to stop worrying? Tell your partner about it.

4. Did you have a difficult time controlling your ejaculation response in some of the positions, men? Was it hard for you to try this many positions and not ejaculate? Did you take breaks?

5. As a couple, did you find a couple of new positions that really got you excited?

6. Briefly interview each other and ask a few specific questions about anything connected with the different positions that might be concerning you.

An Evening of Lovemaking

Every couple is different when it comes to lovemaking. This is about learning new things but with your particular needs and interests in mind. Do what works for you, but remember to try some of the new things in this book so that you keep learning and growing. That's what it's all about and that is why you bought this book.

As your final lesson, co-create a ritual evening together that combines some of your favorite things from the book. Go back to Chapter 6 and read some of the ideas there. You may want to start with a long bath and champagne.

However you design your evening, make sure that you start by harmonizing your energies. Incorporate breathing, eye gazing, and touch into the beginning of your evening. Short erotic massages, even just ten minutes for each of you, will get you present.

You can try a whole new set of positions this time. If you are careful, you may even want to try a standing position or maybe use the couch or an overstuffed chair to try variations of a favorite new position. Use your imagination. If one of you is more used to being the leader, let the other lead this time. You can trade leadership next time.

◀ A ritual lovemaking scene

Sexual dates are very cost-effective entertainment. Design one sexual date a month for yourselves and change the creative atmosphere as often as you can. Hang shawls, sarongs, scarves, and light fabrics on the walls and drape them over the lights. Light candles. Find new music that is evocative and perhaps sounds a little Middle Eastern, much like the followers of the Kama Sutra might have listened to. Create a set and setting that will arouse, delight, and inspire your senses. Ｅ

Chapter 20

Ⓔ **Becoming an Exotic, Erotic Lover**

When all is said and done, it's not technique that makes the great lover; it's presence. Feeling passionate, trusting, and loving yourself are very important. When you bring these qualities and great new techniques to the bedroom, you have a winning formula for life.

Putting It All Together

Nothing is truer than this statement from the Kama Sutra: "Once the wheel of Love has been set in motion, there is no absolute rule" (Part 2, Chapter 2, Sutra 32). There is no holding back when passion and desire fuel your actions, but learning some of the things presented in this book will become a part of who you are, and will affect your love life and the way you interact with your lover.

When you encourage personal growth in your life, you are always expanding on and improving upon what has transpired already in your life. The desire to come back to your true self blossoms, and the search for more meaning in life becomes a force that begs notice in your life.

FACT

The word *Tantra* is a Sanskrit word that means "to weave all of life." Tantra was practiced in ancient India during the time of the Kama Sutra and was the supreme practice of the art of consciousness. It used meditation, yoga, initiation by a guru, secret symbols, and sexuality as the vehicles for life transformation.

The Fabric of Life

Consciousness involves looking at the subtle aspects of your day-to-day experiences as well as the bigger picture that life presents you. Life is like a piece of fabric with a warp and a weft—the object is to "weave" the fabric of life into the finest cloth you can imagine. You can "weave" that beautiful fabric of your life with inspiration, love, pleasure, a conscious mind, compassion, and all the myriad different threads you will bring to your cloth.

The Kama Sutra uses sexuality as a vehicle for transforming what you might normally do without thinking into a more sublime lesson plan for life's fulfillment and enhancement. When you bring consciousness and subtlety to the sexual act, you can make breakthroughs that are profound. More ecstatic energy will be available in your sensual life and in all the other areas of life that you cultivate, too.

Honor the Male and the Female

Look for the good in people and in your partner. In a sense, your partner is your "guru." Simply honoring the woman, the female principle, as the universal goddess and the man, the male principle, as the universal god, helps to bring this into your lives. When you see these divine qualities in your partner and yourself, you begin to see these qualities in everyone and everything in your life.

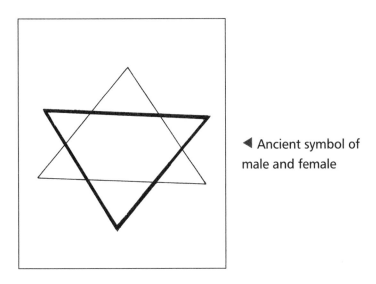

◀ Ancient symbol of male and female

Enjoying Your Own Passion

According to the Kama Sutra, pleasure is one of the three aims of life. The pleasure starts in your own body, so learn to enjoy your own erotic passion and you'll be happy all your life. Building upon your knowledge of your body's pleasure capacity will bridge the gaps that make you doubt your passion.

The keys are in your breath, health, movement, play, practice, and willingness to expand your sensual self. Notice often what you like about yourself. Breathe deeply into those thoughts, almost like a mini meditation, so that you'll remember them and have access to them during the times when you don't feel as well.

It's All About You

Many of the exercises outlined in this book do not require you to have a partner. Be creative, and adapt the exercises to your needs by finding a friend to do them with, using a mirror as your partner, or simply imagining the partner you desire. Use your own intuitive self as a springboard for learning, if you aren't currently partnered.

Practice what you love passionately. Many people worry that they'll be "too big" and that others won't like them for being that way. Be fully yourself as often as you can. Allow others the same space to show up "big" as well—especially your partner.

Create the possibility of deeper connection, more intimacy, sensuality, and more satisfying sex by expanding your capacity to have pleasure. When you bring a whole individual, yourself, to the world, the world recognizes you. You are empowered and attractive when you have balance and are happy in your life. This attractiveness draws a partner to you. You will call forth a partner and lover who is your equal in interests and life philosophy.

Creating Intimacy

Having a deep, intimate connection in your love life is about trusting yourself and your partner. When you give yourself over to vulnerable, open, playful sexuality—that gently pushes your edges and keeps you taking gentle risks—you see how sweet and easy deepening intimacy can be. Doing things together does not necessarily equal intimacy. It's the quality of the time you spend together that counts.

Compassion

No one is perfect. You will never find a perfect person so you can stop wasting your time thinking you will. Often, especially as time passes in a love relationship, you begin to get irritated about little things that didn't bother you before. You can struggle with these things or you can ask yourself: "How are these things related to me and how I act or what I do in this relationship?" By doing this creative thinking, you can begin to have compassion for your partner and for yourself.

ALERT!

Taking time to talk about goals, problems, work, home, or whatever it is that your life is about is very important. Listening to each other attentively and thoughtfully will make your partner feel loved. It is one of the greatest gifts you can give and it doesn't cost a dime.

Vulnerability

Being truly vulnerable with your partner could be the hardest thing you ever do—whether you are a woman or a man. Men aren't very experienced at being vulnerable, and women don't often trust enough to think they will be heard.

If this is hard for you, start with easy disclosures about yourself. Maybe something that hurt you as a child or something that happened to you in your family that made you feel unworthy of attention could be safe enough to begin with. Whatever it is, speak in "I" statements and speak about your feelings. When you talk about feelings and don't blame others, the listener's heart opens up automatically.

Playfulness

Do more creative things together, even if it feels silly sometimes. Erotic writing, creating love rituals together, designing an erotic evening, breathing together before a sexual encounter, or even practicing PC muscle exercises together are activities that will add tremendously to your love life, as well as to your everyday life. You might want to systematically explore all the different types of positions, have blindfolded touch and pleasuring rituals, or create a situation where you can have sex outside the bedroom. The living room furniture, love-swings, and piles of pillows make what could be an ordinary evening into an extraordinary one.

Don't forget to be playful all the time. Find things to do that engage the two of you to work or create together. Gardening, walks in nature, getting away together, or going to the zoo or a museum are all much more intimate and stimulating than sitting next to each other watching television.

Gently Pushing the Edges

Building trust in a relationship is of the highest importance. If trust is lacking you can't expect either of you to try fun, exciting new things, especially in the bedroom. Vulnerability helps create trust.

Trust is necessary to explore adventurous new things together. Remember, too, that it's good to stay open to trying but if something doesn't work for you, say so to your partner. Discuss openly how you might modify or change the thing to fit both of your needs. Keep pushing those edges, though, to grow and expand with your lover.

Communicating

Knowing what you want from a lover and being able to ask for it are two very important things in any relationship. You need to know what you want, before you can ask for it effectively, though. The next exercise is a wonderful combination of both.

Scenario #1: A couple is in the bedroom and they've been kissing and warming up to a potential hot evening. Her blouse comes off and he is going for her nipples. He's excited, but his touch is too rough. She's not ready for this. She blurts out, "Ouch, that's too hard." He backs away and they share a moment of very awkward silence. He rolls on his back and turns away—well—you can see where this is going.

Scenario #2: A couple is in the bedroom and they've been kissing and warming up to a potential lovemaking. Her blouse comes off and he is going for her nipples. He's excited, but his touch is too rough. She's not ready for this. She says, "Oh, I love my nipples fondled. Could you try touching them lightly with just your fingertips?" He immediately tries this because he feels acknowledged and not chastised. She likes her nipples fondled—she just needs it done with a lighter touch. She says, "*Mmm . . . that's perfect.*"

ALERT!

If your communication with your partner isn't good, don't expect that your sex life will get better. Communicating, listening, and telling what hurts you are prerequisites to great sex. When this area of your life is healed, your sex life will get much, much better.

Communication Structure

By using a simple communication structure to ask for the kind of touch and loving you need, you will also learn what you actually want and need. Here is how this simple structure works:

1. Acknowledge something you like.
2. Ask for a single change.
3. Acknowledge the change.

It's that simple. Look back at the second scenario and see just how the three steps fit in. At step 3 you may find that you were just experimenting and you didn't care for the change. You could then say, "Gosh, I thought I'd like that, but it didn't work as well as I thought it might." You could then go back to step 2 and ask for another single change. "Honey, could you try touching my whole breast?" Then, "Yessss . . . That's great." This helps both of you get better at defining your likes, wants, and desires in a nonblame way.

Use It Everywhere

The use of this easy communication structure can take as many forms as you can think of for it. You'll use examples from the sensual and sexual context to practice it, but this style of communication can be used with your children, your boss, your employees, your friends, your mother, your neighbor, or your lover. By using it, you'll be able to discover what you like and what you don't like, and you'll empower your lover to freely give you what you want and ask for what he or she wants, too.

Timing During Lovemaking

Getting creative with the timing of the positions you use during lovemaking will make all the difference in the quality of the experience. When you begin in certain postures and then move through to others, the woman begins to be aroused and the man can maintain his excitement without going over the top too soon. Learn to feel your way in this dance of love.

If you want your woman to be an erotic partner, focus your love on her needs first and be attentive. Tease and play, and open up your woman to the possibilities of her own erotic nature and then stand back!

Arousal and Foreplay

The Kama Sutra and many other Asian love manuals from the past say that the woman's passions are slow to arousal. Once she is there though, she is hot and can often go beyond her partner in duration of the sex act. The great lover knows this and practices techniques to get her aroused and ready for each step in the lovemaking journey.

Many women don't feel empowered enough to educate their lovers on this fact. It's a very big reason that women lose interest in sex and go begrudgingly to the bedroom to fulfill their duties. They aren't being aroused, have had a history of not being aroused, and can't find ways to step up to the plate to get what they need for arousal.

Timing of the Position Dance

On the other side of the coin, women need to help their men last longer so that they will enjoy every bit of the long, luxurious ride during intercourse. Don't think you are powerful and talented if you get him "off" too fast. That is not the point here.

Ejaculation mastery will train him not only to last a long time, but it will give him the immense pleasure of having multiple peaks and experiences during a single sexual encounter. This is imperative if you want to dance through many position changes. Some positions are better than others to start with, and others are better when you want to sustain the energy and not go over the top too soon.

Generally positions that put a lot of friction and stimulus on the lingam and yoni may be good for the woman to start intercourse in, but they won't be so great for the man unless he has mastered his ejaculation. Form a circle with your thumb and index finger with the fingertips touching. Now put the index finger of your other hand in and out of this circle. Notice that when you go straight in and out, your fingers hardly touch.

Now, doing this same exercise, move the finger that is going in and out to an extreme angle—for example upward—so that the tip of that finger is pointing toward the fingers on the hand that is forming the circle. What happens? There's a lot more friction, isn't there? The friction is on the man's lingam and that friction is in just the right spot for the woman's G-spot.

◀ Timing can be everything when trying a new position.

Keep eye contact so that the two of you can be in communication, even if it isn't verbal at that moment. This helps a lot. Often women who have been doing their PC muscle sexercises for a while can really feel the lingam inside them. They can tell when their partner is getting too far along, and they can slow down or stop the movement so that the two of them can just breathe and relax for a few minutes. This is the perfect time for both of you to pump your love muscles and relax.

Controlling Ejaculation

To last longer, try positions that give the man a lot of control in the movement of his pelvis. The Modified Yab/Yum Position where the man sits on the side of the bed or on a hassock and the woman sits on his lap, facing him, is good for ejaculation control and for hitting the G-spot in the woman. Another good one is for the woman to be lying back on the edge of the bed and the man to stand while he is inside her. He can hold her legs or feet in the air or she can hold her own legs. This one gives the man great control over his timing and rhythm.

FACT

Relaxing positions, like the Spooning and Clasping Positions, are good for men who are trying to last longer. There's less friction and a relaxing mode is always helpful for control.

Timing of Orgasms

There are many types of orgasms and blends of orgasms, for both the man and the woman, but timing them so that everyone gets to have at least one is sometimes difficult. Creating the opportunity for the woman to have a clitoral orgasm first before intercourse is one way to accomplish this. Often this will lead to her being able to have a second or third vaginal orgasm during intercourse, too.

Some men have a more difficult time having an orgasm than others. This is great for prolonged sex, but not very satisfying for the man who feels as though he can't let go into the orgasmic bliss. For this man, use positions that feel empowering and experiment with new, exciting positions, too. Women, touch them lovingly and use your hands to brush the sexual energy into their heart area to remind them that they are loved and that they can relax and let go.

The ultimate is to have orgasms together, at the same time. This is something that is difficult for most couples and isn't necessary for lovemaking. Still, in the adventure of sex, it is something that can be easily accomplished if you are seasoned lovers and take the time to develop the capacity for it.

After Making Love

The Kama Sutra suggests that the appropriate etiquette for the glow after making love is to bask in each other's arms and to speak words of love to each other. Men are cautioned to pay particular attention to this part of the act of lovemaking. Spooning positions are excellent for this time. Caresses, kisses, and sweet wishes spoken to each other bring a sense of trust and warmth that is valuable to the emotional health of the couple.

QUESTION?

What's your favorite way to end a lovemaking experience? Ask your lover and each of you tell your favorite endings. Be descriptive and creative, but tell the truth. Try each other's suggestions out soon.

Your memories are created and retained through your emotional reactions to what is happening. This is true for everything we do in life. Sweet emotional reactions are recorded in your memory banks and support positive response for the future.

Connecting the Heart and the Genitals

The Chinese art of lovemaking through the Taoist's perspective has an old saying that goes something like this: Women's energy comes from the heavens and moves to the earth and men's energy comes from the earth and moves toward the heavens. In other words—open a woman's heart first and then her legs will open; open a man's legs first and then his heart will open.

If we could all just remember this and not take it personally, when we are refused what we think we need, the world of men and women would work better. Each of us must move closer to the other's point of view and create ways to meet our needs. Create a dance of love between the two of you that shares the duties and the privileges of a wonderful sex life.

Creating more connection between the heart and the genitals can be easy. During sex, women can brush the sexual energy toward their lover's heart to remind him to feel the connection. Men can hold their lover in their arms and lightly touch her heart and her yoni. Put intention into your hearts for the healing of the differences.

Appendices

Appendix A

Resource Guide

Appendix B

Glossary

Appendix A

Resource Guide

Burton, Sir Richard, *The Kama Sutra of Vatsyayana,* (New York: Barnes and Noble, 1995).

Burton, Sir Richard, and F. F. Arbuthnot, *The Illustrated Kama Sutra, Ananga Ranga, and Perfumed Garden,* (Rochester, VT: Park Street Press, 1987).

Danielou, Alain, *The Complete Kama Sutra,* (Rochester, VT: Park Street Press, 1994).

De Luca, Diana, *Botanica Erotica: Arousing Body, Mind, and Spirit,* (Rochester, VT: Healing Arts Press, 1998).

Douglas, Nik, and Penny Slinger, *Sexual Secrets: The Alchemy of Ecstasy,* (Rochester, VT: Destiny Books, 1979).

Heumann, Suzie, and Susan Campbell Ph.D., *The Everything® Great Sex Book,* (Avon, MA: Adams Media, 2004).

Upadhyaya, S. C., *Kama Sutra of Vatsyayana,* (Bombay, India: D. B. Taraporevala Sons and Company, Ltd., 1961).

Wikoff, Johanina, Ph.D., and Deborah S. Romaine, *The Complete Idiot's Guide to the Kama Sutra,* (Indianapolis, IN: Pearson Education Comp., 2000).

Glossary

aphrodisiac: A substance, words, or actions that stimulate the desire for passionate, intimate contact.

Artha: One of the four aims of life; the term for the acquisition of wealth as a duty to one's family and to life's pursuits. One must be able to support oneself and a family comfortably in order to have time to pursue pleasure and holy duties, which were required of a good citizen.

asana: A posture or position in yoga or meditation.

Brahman: The highest of the Hindu castes. They are often holy men or kings.

Burton, Sir Richard: Englishman who translated the Kama Sutra in 1838 from the Sanskrit original.

chakras: "Wheels" of energy or energy centers in the body that correspond to points in the body that move energy up the spine. The chakras represent emotional and psychological factors that correspond to a hierarchy of personal growth.

courtesan: A sacred prostitute, usually well educated in many subjects but especially the art of love.

Dharma: One of the four aims in life; good, upstanding actions and the following of religious principles and doctrines of the Hindu philosophy.

frenulum: The sensitive ridge around the lip of the head of the penis and on the underside, specifically.

Kama: One of the four aims of life; pleasure, sensual sexuality, love, also the God of Love.

Khajuraho: A small village in northern India that still contains about twenty of the original eighty-five erotic temples built between A.D. 950–1050.

lingam: A Sanskrit word for the male genitals; the penis, and the universal ancient symbol of the male creative principle.

mantra: A magical prayer often given by a guru to the student. There are also many famous mantras that can be recited for the specific purpose they address.

Moksha: The last of the four aims of life; the liberation from the cycle of birth and death that the Hindu religion believes occurs to humans. If humans live by the three aims of Artha, Dharma, and Kama, then they will decrease the amount of times they will need to be reborn before they can reach Moksha, or Nirvana.

sage: A wise elder, often a wanderer.

Sanskrit: The ancient scholarly language that the Kama Sutra was originally written in.

shakti: The universal feminine principle that is in everything. She was the consort and lover of Shiva. Together they form the principle of yin/yang, the universal male/female balance in the world.

shiva: The universal male principle that is in everything. He was the consort and lover of Shakti.

sutra: Aphorisms, short rules or lessons.

tantra: The profound study of one's nature and relationship to everything in life and the universe. Often in the company of a guru, a student would be guided in the intimate study of himself and the transcendence possible. Strenuous personal work is required to catapult one to a state of enlightenment.

Taoism: A Chinese system of health, long life, and internally focused body-based practices that promote balance and connection with the natural scheme of life.

Vatsyayana: The ancient scholar who transcribed and shortened, with his own notations, the original Kama Shastras text to the Kama Sutra verses we know today. By best estimates it's thought that he did this work some time around A.D. 300–400.

vulva: The external genital organs of the female, including the labia, clitoris, and vestibule of the vagina.

yantra: A magical shape, picture, or representation. A symbol.

yoga: A system of breathing, positions, and body/health disciplines that promote unity of the individual with a higher, supreme being.

yoni: A Sanskrit word for the feminine genitals; the vulva and vagina, and the universal ancient symbol of the feminine regenerative principle.

Index

THE EVERYTHING SERIES!

BUSINESS

Everything® Business Planning Book
Everything® Coaching and Mentoring Book
Everything® Fundraising Book
Everything® Home-Based Business Book
Everything® Landlording Book
Everything® Leadership Book
Everything® Managing People Book
Everything® Negotiating Book
Everything® Online Business Book
Everything® Project Management Book
Everything® Robert's Rules Book, $7.95
Everything® Selling Book
Everything® Start Your Own Business Book
Everything® Time Management Book

COMPUTERS

Everything® Computer Book

COOKBOOKS

Everything® Barbecue Cookbook
Everything® Bartender's Book, $9.95
Everything® Chinese Cookbook
Everything® Chocolate Cookbook
Everything® Cookbook
Everything® Dessert Cookbook
Everything® Diabetes Cookbook
Everything® Fondue Cookbook
Everything® Grilling Cookbook
Everything® Holiday Cookbook
Everything® Indian Cookbook
Everything® Low-Carb Cookbook
Everything® Low-Fat High-Flavor Cookbook
Everything® Low-Salt Cookbook
Everything® Mediterranean Cookbook
Everything® Mexican Cookbook
Everything® One-Pot Cookbook
Everything® Pasta Cookbook
Everything® Quick Meals Cookbook
Everything® Slow Cooker Cookbook
Everything® Soup Cookbook

Everything® Thai Cookbook
Everything® Vegetarian Cookbook
Everything® Wine Book

HEALTH

Everything® Alzheimer's Book
Everything® Anti-Aging Book
Everything® Diabetes Book
Everything® Dieting Book
Everything® Hypnosis Book
Everything® Low Cholesterol Book
Everything® Massage Book
Everything® Menopause Book
Everything® Nutrition Book
Everything® Reflexology Book
Everything® Reiki Book
Everything® Stress Management Book
Everything® Vitamins, Minerals, and
       Nutritional Supplements Book

HISTORY

Everything® American Government Book
Everything® American History Book
Everything® Civil War Book
Everything® Irish History & Heritage Book
Everything® Mafia Book
Everything® Middle East Book

HOBBIES & GAMES

Everything® Bridge Book
Everything® Candlemaking Book
Everything® Card Games Book
Everything® Cartooning Book
Everything® Casino Gambling Book, 2nd Ed.
Everything® Chess Basics Book
Everything® Crossword and Puzzle Book
Everything® Crossword Challenge Book
Everything® Drawing Book
Everything® Digital Photography Book
Everything® Easy Crosswords Book
Everything® Family Tree Book

Everything® Games Book
Everything® Knitting Book
Everything® Magic Book
Everything® Motorcycle Book
Everything® Online Genealogy Book
Everything® Photography Book
Everything® Poker Strategy Book
Everything® Pool & Billiards Book
Everything® Quilting Book
Everything® Scrapbooking Book
Everything® Sewing Book
Everything® Soapmaking Book

HOME IMPROVEMENT

Everything® Feng Shui Book
Everything® Feng Shui Decluttering Book, $9.95
Everything® Fix-It Book
Everything® Homebuilding Book
Everything® Home Decorating Book
Everything® Landscaping Book
Everything® Lawn Care Book
Everything® Organize Your Home Book

EVERYTHING® KIDS' BOOKS

All titles are $6.95

Everything® Kids' Baseball Book, 3rd Ed.
Everything® Kids' Bible Trivia Book
Everything® Kids' Bugs Book
Everything® Kids' Christmas Puzzle
    & Activity Book
Everything® Kids' Cookbook
Everything® Kids' Halloween Puzzle
    & Activity Book
Everything® Kids' Hidden Pictures Book
    Everything® Kids' Joke Book
Everything® Kids' Knock Knock Book
Everything® Kids' Math Puzzles Book
Everything® Kids' Mazes Book
Everything® Kids' Money Book

All Everything® books are priced at $12.95 or $14.95, unless otherwise stated. Prices subject to change without notice.

Everything® Kids' Monsters Book
Everything® Kids' Nature Book
Everything® Kids' Puzzle Book
Everything® Kids' Riddles & Brain Teasers Book
Everything® Kids' Science Experiments Book
Everything® Kids' Soccer Book
Everything® Kids' Travel Activity Book

KIDS' STORY BOOKS

Everything® Bedtime Story Book
Everything® Bible Stories Book
Everything® Fairy Tales Book

LANGUAGE

Everything® Conversational Japanese Book
    (with CD), $19.95
Everything® Inglés Book
Everything® French Phrase Book, $9.95
Everything® Learning French Book
Everything® Learning German Book
Everything® Learning Italian Book
Everything® Learning Latin Book
Everything® Learning Spanish Book
Everything® Sign Language Book
Everything® Spanish Phrase Book, $9.95
Everything® Spanish Verb Book, $9.95

MUSIC

Everything® Drums Book (with CD), $19.95
Everything® Guitar Book
Everything® Home Recording Book
Everything® Playing Piano and Keyboards Book
Everything® Rock & Blues Guitar Book
    (with CD), $19.95
Everything® Songwriting Book

NEW AGE

Everything® Astrology Book
Everything® Dreams Book
Everything® Ghost Book
Everything® Love Signs Book, $9.95
Everything® Meditation Book
Everything® Numerology Book
Everything® Paganism Book
Everything® Palmistry Book
Everything® Psychic Book
Everything® Spells & Charms Book
Everything® Tarot Book
Everything® Wicca and Witchcraft Book

PARENTING

Everything® Baby Names Book
Everything® Baby Shower Book
Everything® Baby's First Food Book
Everything® Baby's First Year Book
Everything® Birthing Book
Everything® Breastfeeding Book
Everything® Father-to-Be Book
Everything® Get Ready for Baby Book
Everything® Getting Pregnant Book
Everything® Homeschooling Book
Everything® Parent's Guide to Children
    with Asperger's Syndrome
Everything® Parent's Guide to Children
    with Autism
Everything® Parent's Guide to Children
    with Dyslexia
Everything® Parent's Guide to Positive Discipline
Everything® Parent's Guide to Raising a
    Successful Child
Everything® Parenting a Teenager Book
Everything® Potty Training Book, $9.95
Everything® Pregnancy Book, 2nd Ed.
Everything® Pregnancy Fitness Book
Everything® Pregnancy Nutrition Book
Everything® Pregnancy Organizer, $15.00
Everything® Toddler Book
Everything® Tween Book

PERSONAL FINANCE

Everything® Budgeting Book
Everything® Get Out of Debt Book
Everything® Homebuying Book, 2nd Ed.
Everything® Homeselling Book
Everything® Investing Book
Everything® Online Business Book
Everything® Personal Finance Book
Everything® Personal Finance in Your
    20s & 30s Book
Everything® Real Estate Investing Book
Everything® Wills & Estate Planning Book

PETS

Everything® Cat Book
Everything® Dog Book
Everything® Dog Training and Tricks Book
Everything® Golden Retriever Book
Everything® Horse Book
Everything® Labrador Retriever Book
Everything® Poodle Book

Everything® Puppy Book
Everything® Rottweiler Book
Everything® Tropical Fish Book

REFERENCE

Everything® Car Care Book
Everything® Classical Mythology Book
Everything® Einstein Book
Everything® Etiquette Book
Everything® Great Thinkers Book
Everything® Philosophy Book
Everything® Psychology Book
Everything® Shakespeare Book
Everything® Toasts Book

RELIGION

Everything® Angels Book
Everything® Bible Book
Everything® Buddhism Book
Everything® Catholicism Book
Everything® Christianity Book
Everything® Jewish History & Heritage Book
Everything® Judaism Book
Everything® Koran Book
Everything® Prayer Book
Everything® Saints Book
Everything® Understanding Islam Book
Everything® World's Religions Book
Everything® Zen Book

SCHOOL & CAREERS

Everything® After College Book
Everything® Alternative Careers Book
Everything® College Survival Book
Everything® Cover Letter Book
Everything® Get-a-Job Book
Everything® Job Interview Book
Everything® New Teacher Book
Everything® Online Job Search Book
Everything® Personal Finance Book
Everything® Practice Interview Book
Everything® Resume Book, 2nd Ed.
Everything® Study Book

SELF-HELP/ RELATIONSHIPS

Everything® Dating Book
Everything® Divorce Book
Everything® Great Sex Book

All Everything® books are priced at $12.95 or $14.95, unless otherwise stated. Prices subject to change without notice.

Everything® Kama Sutra Book
Everything® Self-Esteem Book

SPORTS & FITNESS

Everything® Body Shaping Book
Everything® Fishing Book
Everything® Fly-Fishing Book
Everything® Golf Book
Everything® Golf Instruction Book
Everything® Knots Book
Everything® Pilates Book
Everything® Running Book
Everything® T'ai Chi and QiGong Book
Everything® Total Fitness Book
Everything® Weight Training Book
Everything® Yoga Book

TRAVEL

Everything® Family Guide to Hawaii
Everything® Family Guide to New York City,
　　2nd Ed.

Everything® Family Guide to Washington D.C.,
　　2nd Ed.
Everything® Family Guide to the Walt Disney
　　World Resort®, Universal Studios®,
　　and Greater Orlando, 4th Ed.
Everything® Guide to Las Vegas
Everything® Guide to New England
Everything® Travel Guide to the Disneyland
　　Resort®, California Adventure®,
　　Universal Studios®, and the
　　Anaheim Area

WEDDINGS

Everything® Bachelorette Party Book, $9.95
Everything® Bridesmaid Book, $9.95
Everything® Creative Wedding Ideas Book
Everything® Elopement Book, $9.95
Everything® Father of the Bride Book, $9.95
Everything® Groom Book, $9.95
Everything® Jewish Wedding Book
Everything® Mother of the Bride Book, $9.95
Everything® Wedding Book, 3rd Ed.

Everything® Wedding Checklist, $7.95
Everything® Wedding Etiquette Book, $7.95
Everything® Wedding Organizer, $15.00
Everything® Wedding Shower Book, $7.95
Everything® Wedding Vows Book, $7.95
Everything® Weddings on a Budget Book, $9.95

WRITING

Everything® Creative Writing Book
Everything® Get Published Book
Everything® Grammar and Style Book
Everything® Grant Writing Book
Everything® Guide to Writing a Novel
Everything® Guide to Writing Children's Books
Everything® Screenwriting Book
Everything® Writing Well Book

Introducing an exceptional new line of beginner craft books from the Everything® series!

All titles are $14.95.

Everything® Crafts—Create Your Own Greeting Cards
1-59337-226-4
Everything® Crafts—Polymer Clay for Beginners
1-59337-230-2

Everything® Crafts—Rubberstamping Made Easy
1-59337-229-9
Everything® Crafts—Wedding Decorations
and Keepsakes
1-59337-227-2

Available wherever books are sold!
To order, call 800-872-5627, or visit us at *www.everything.com*
Everything® and everything.com® are registered trademarks of F+W Publications, Inc.